Preface.

If the reader expects to find highly wrought sentimentality or romantic fancies in the succeeding pages, he had better lay them down, and seek for gratification elsewhere. But if a desire to learn somewhat of the stern realities of rugged life, and to profit by timely cautions, animates the heart, then the author can cordially invite his reader to a more intimate acquaintanceship. Time is too short, the purposes of life are too exalted, and the dangers of human existence too fearful, to admit of any trifling, even on the festival of marriage. Marriage is not a small matter, however lightly its solemn vows may escape from thoughtless lips. Nay, its influences are "great for good or for evil, because of the unfathomable mysteries that lie shrouded in the growth on earth of an immortal soul." Happiness or woe, heaven or hell, will issue from the marriage covenant. It would, therefore, most surely be out of place to present the "contracting parties" with aught that would weaken their ideas concerning the responsibility of their new relation.

Deeply impressed with these truths, I have prayerfully written this little work.

BRIDAL GREETINGS:

A Marriage Gift,

IN WHICH THE MUTUAL DUTIES OF HUSBAND
AND WIFE ARE FAMILIARLY ILLUSTRATED
AND ENFORCED.

BY REV. DANIEL WISE,

Author of "The Path of Life, "Christian Love," etc.

MARRIAGE IS THE MOTHER OF THE WORLD, AND PRE-
SERVES KINGDOMS, AND FILLS CITIES, AND CHURCHES,
AND HEAVEN ITSELF.—JEREMY TAYLOR.
LADY, THY MARRIAGE-BELLS ARE RINGING.—MRS. ABDY

New-York:
PUBLISHED BY CARLTON & PHILLIPS,
200 MULBERRY-STREET.
1852.

Entered according to Act of Congress, in the year 1850

BY LANE & SCOTT,

in the Clerk's Office of the District Court of the Southern District of New-York.

I have aimed to make every sentence *profitable* to the reader; yet, in doing this, I have sought to give interest and vivacity to grave truths by illustrations drawn from real experience; for, to use the lines of Tasso:—

> "So the fond mother her sick infant blinds,
> Sprinkling the edges of the cup she gives
> With sweets; delighted with the balm it finds
> Round the sweet brim, the medicine it receives,—
> Drinks the delusive draught, and, thus deluded, lives."

Trusting that I shall hereby contribute to the real and final happiness of the newly married, I confide the result of my labours to the keeping of Christ, without whose blessing it will prove but a fruitless effort.

Let the reader, in perusing my

thoughts, do as I have done in writing them—seek light and grace to profit, at the throne of Infinite Wisdom; and then reader and author will have occasion to rejoice in eternity over their mutual acquaintance.   D. **WISE.**

Fall River, Mass., 1849.

Contents.

CHAPTER I.

GREETINGS AND CAUTIONS.

Address to the Bride—Blended Images—Solemnity proper on Wedding Occasions—Goethe—Jeremy Taylor—Poetical Extract—The Bride's Strength—Good wishes of Friends—Extract from Barry Cornwall—The Bridegroom addressed—A Wish from Vaughn—Address to both Bride and Bridegroom—Social Happiness must be sought—Montgomery to the newly Wedded—An inexperienced Youth—Unsuspected Folly—Hope the Genius of most Marriages—Extravagant Expectations of Happiness discouraged—Sorrow the Destiny of all—Extract on human Pleasures—Dr. Fuller—A Question and its Answer . . . . Page 13

CHAPTER II.

ON AVOIDING THE FIRST QUARREL.

Only one dangerous Quarrel in Married Life—Bridal Incredulity—Effect of the first Quarrel—Courtship and its Influence on Married Life—The Honey-moon—Discoveries—The crisis of Conjugal Bliss—Influence of Trifles—Jeremy Taylor on beginning Right—The Boiled Egg and the Testy Bride—The offended Bridegroom—The Quarrel—The Separation—How to avoid the Danger 23

CHAPTER III.

OF BEGINNING MARRIED LIFE RELIGIOUSLY.

Marriage is a Divine Institution—Consistent with Religious Enjoyment—Scruples—Fletcher's Scruples—His Spirituality in the Married State—Fletcher's Argument against his own Scruples—The Holiest Persons have been Married—Possibility of Religion in the Married State shown—Marriage too frequently an Occasion of Sin—Unnecessary—A common Excuse for not Erecting a Family Altar—The Bridal Home should be Consecrated to God—The Benefits of such a Dedication—Tertullian—Public Worship—Sabbath Arrangements—Domestics and the Sabbath—A Rule recommended—The Daring of those who Marry irreligiously—The Tree—An Irreligious Home will become Joyless—A Lamentation over such—Exhortation to Marry Christ—Consolation in thoughts of Reunion—Simon Marechal and his Heroic Wife . . . . Page 32

CHAPTER IV.

OF RELIGIOUS DIFFERENCES.

The Bride and Bridegroom belonging to different Persuasions—A Danger—Avoidable—Compromise recommended—Submission and Union urged—Husband's rights over the Children—One of the Parties unconverted—Serious Difficulty—Duty of the Christian thus circumstanced—The chief Object—How to Succeed—Emily Churchill—Her Experience—Marriage—Her Mind revived—The Effort—An encouraging Fact—The Scoffer's Conversion—His confession—Domestic Persecutions—Robert Willis and his bitter Wife—All domestic Persecution contemptible—The Sea of Life viewed—Tasso's Pilot—The best Way . . . . Page 45

CHAPTER V.

OF RELATIVES AND FRIENDS.

The Future—A Prize—New Relations—The stepmother and Maiden Sister—The Wife a Queen in her Home—A melancholy Example—Madame Guion and her Step-mother—Madame Guion's Misery—Cautions in regard to Relatives—Old Friends—How to be treated—An ideal Picture—Henrietta and Henry Burgess—An important Lesson—Some old Friendships to be discontinued—Confidants unnecessary to Married Persons—Sad Effects—Mutual and Entire Confidence recommended—Extract from Tupper—An impropriety described . . . 68

CHAPTER VI.

HOME AND ITS ARRANGEMENTS.

A Home needed—Its Character not dependent on its Cost—Forethought Needful—Wisdom of the Swallow—An Etching—The unwise Housekeepers—The two Tenements—Expensive Furniture—Increased Expenses—Business Embarrassments—Insolvency—Misery—Poor Richard's saying—Simple Rules—Expenditures and Income—Expense Account—Prudent Calculations—Covetousness Deprecated—Necessity for Saving illustrated—On giving Parties—The new Sofa—The Girandoles—The Party—Ellen's Chagrin—Remarks on Parties—Independent Action urged—Cheap Purchases—Sayings of Franklin . 84

CHAPTER VII.

ON MAKING HOME HAPPY.

The first Year of Married Life important—Conjugal Love a delicate Plant—The *spirit* makes the home—The eccentric Bridegroom—The Philosophy of a happy Home—Motto on a Wedding Ring—Selfishness must be avoided—Extract from Dr. Wayland—Conrad and Matilda—Catharine Adorna—Her Conquest of a Selfish Husband—The Husband must supply the Wants of his Family liberally—Indolent Husbands censured—Alexander and Maria—Fretting and Scolding—The fretful Husband—The complaining Wife—Dante and his wife Gemma—Rousseau on Empire of Woman—Beautiful Extract—Solomon—Bishop Patrick—Mrs. Hemans—The Vaudois Wife to her Husband . . . . . . Page 103

CHAPTER VIII.

ON CONFORMITY TO CIRCUMSTANCES.

The Pastor's Visit—The Home-sick Wife—Her Folly—A Contrast—Mrs. Pickard—Her admirable Self-denial—The discontented Wife—The Clergyman's Bride—John Wesley's Wife—Catharine Von Bora—Which does the Bride admire?—Minister's Wife must enter into the Spirit of his Profession—The high Character of his Mission—Heroism under Trials—Illustration—Appeal to the Minister's Bride—A touching Exhibition of Conjugal respect—A Hint for Husbands—Sympathy for a Wife the Husband's duty—Mountford on Sympathy—How the Husband must Sympathize—Poetical Extract . . . 125

CHAPTER IX.

OF DOMESTIC SERVANTS.

Servants great Plagues—Abraham and Lot—The Relation an effect of Sin—Best to Dispense with Help—The Expense of keeping Help considered—Extract—Bad Temper of hired Help—Its Effect on Family Happiness—Sad Influence of wicked Servants on Children—Folly of keeping Help for Fashion sake—Poor Health makes Help needful for some—Pious Servants are Family Jewels—Catholic Help—May we keep Such if they will not attend Family Prayer?—Question of Priestly dictation considered—How to do Good to Catholic Help—General Principles of Treatment—Burns—System in House-keeping—The Wife must Superintend in Person—Solomon's Picture of a good Housewife—An illustrative Narrative—Concluding Note . . . Page 146

CHAPTER I.

Greetings and Cautions.

Peace to thee, fair and gentle bride! Thou art now joined to the soul for whom thine was moulded. Blessings rest on thy head, which, in the multitude of its half sad, half joyful thoughts, inclines towards thy chosen one in serious playfulness, drooping

> "as a lily droops
> Faint o'er a folded rose."

I know that the beautiful images of the happy past are blending with the misty dreams of the future in your perplexed mind. Perchance your spirit trembles before the future, or sighs at yielding up the past. It is well to stand thus timidly hopeful in the bridal hour. Unmingled joy, festive song, should not flow unrestrainedly in a crisis teeming with the serenest bliss or the mightiest woe. "Festivities," writes the great German poet, (Goethe,) "are fit for what is happily concluded; at the commencement, they but waste the force and zeal which should inspire us. Of all festivities, the marriage festival appears the most unsuitable; calmness, humility, and silent hope befit no ceremony more than this." I do not blame you, therefore, lady, for the silent tear. "Life or death, felicity or a lasting sorrow, are in the power of marriage," says Jeremy Taylor. Yet yield not thyself wholly to sadness. For though

"Thine is a path by snares and toils attended:
  Yet, lady, in thy prudence I confide;
Thou art not by mere mortal aid befriended,—
  Prayer is thy stay, and Providence thy guide:
And should thy coming years with ills be laden,
  Thou safely may'st abide the storms of life,
If the meek virtues of the Christian maiden
  Shine forth as brightly in the Christian wife."
                                    MRS. ABDY

Courage, then, timid bride! God will go before you into the dreamy future. The prayers of your friends are also your companions. Listen to the silver-toned voices of those beloved ones, whose loving hearts are inspiring their lips with sincere wishes for your future good. Hear them saying, as thou art passing from the home of thy youth:—

> "Sweet be her dreams, the fair, the young;
> Grace, beauty, breathe upon her;
> Music, haunt thou about her tongue;
> Life, fill her path with honour.
>
> "All golden thoughts, all wealth of days,
> Truth, friendship, love surround her;
> So may she smile till life be closed,
> And angel bands have crown'd her."
>
> BARRY CORNWALL.

Peace to thee, also, young bridegroom! The "desire of thine eyes" is now thine own. Deal gently with her; for she has been gently reared, and her heart is a delicate and fragile thing: easily broken. Seek a spiritual union with thy bride, that the strength of thy manhood, blending with the weakness of her woman's nature, may impart vigour to her soul, while she repays thee by throwing gentle refining influences over thy spirit. Thus joined to her in the spirit of true marriage,—

> "Fresh as the hours may all your pleasures be,
> And healthful as eternity;
> Sweet as the flowers' first breath, and close
> As the unseen spreadings of the rose."—VAUGHN.

And peace to you both! May those bright, calm smiles play on your lips forever! May your hearts never be divided, your affections blighted, nor your young hopes blasted! May your life-sun ever shine in unclouded splendour, and your path through the vale of life be green, smooth, and pleasant as love, sanctified by religion, and guided by Providence, can make it!

Such are the greetings that the heart of friendship offers for your acceptance in the bridal hour. They are sincerely laid at your feet. Take them, happy pair, as omens of good. Put them into that beautiful rainbow with which hope has spanned the sky of your married life. Make it your care to convert them into realities by appropriate effort; for, believe me, social happiness is not an accidental guest. It comes not without invitation: it abides not without attention. Woo it, then, to your bridal dwelling; and once there, on your peril, give it no umbrage. Force it not to depart, lest it avenge the slight by sending discord—the bitterest of the daughters of sin—to occupy its place. Do this, and you shall realize the wishes of a great and pure poet, (Montgomery,) who sings thus to the newly wedded:—

"Then may the union of young hearts,
  So early and so well begun,
Like sea and shore, in all their parts,
  Appear as twain, but be as one.

"Be it like summer—may they find
  Bliss, beauty, hope, where'er they roam:
Be it like winter, when confined—
  Peace, comfort, happiness, at home.

"Like day and night—sweet interchange
　Of care, enjoyment, action, rest;
Absence nor coldness e'er estrange
　Hearts by unfailing love possess'd:

"Like earth's horizon—be their scene
　Of life a rich and various ground;
And, whether lowering or serene,
　Heaven all above it and around.

"When land and ocean, day and night,
　When years and nature cease to be,
May their inheritance be light,
　Their union, one eternity."

An inexperienced and thoughtless youth was going a long journey alone. His imagination was excited by visions of pleasure. "Tell me," he cried, "of all the *pleasant* things I shall behold on my journey."

His wiser friends suggested, "There are *dangers* as well as pleasures on your journey."

"Nay," he retorted; "tell me of its pleasant things."

This was folly; because the only way to secure a prosperous journey was to know its dangers, and, by wise precautions, to avoid them.

But obvious as this folly is to an observer, it has multitudes in its chains who do not even suspect, much less feel, their bondage: especially is this true of those who are starting on the laborious and perilous journey of married life.

The bridal day is by most exclusively consecrated to *hope*. Viewed in those sunny hours, the vale of life looks green and fruitful everywhere. The joyous pair see only emerald hills rising " terrace above terrace," smooth walks, peaceful bowers, quiet skies. Hand in hand they walk those paths, linger under those bowers, and smile beneath those cloudless skies in boundless happiness. The past appears as the sterile wilderness did to the weary sons of Abraham—the future as a Canaan of unmingled delight.

Alas! these hopes are doomed to dimness and decay. I would not needlessly evoke a cloud to darken this prospect of bliss. I would not ruthlessly and unkindly dash this cup of bliss from those youthful lips. I will not even affirm that moderate bridal hopes cannot grow into fruition. But I would teach the newly married that extravagant expectations will be sure to meet with bitter disappointments. I would have them understand that storms do obscure the skies; that floods do overflow the vale of married life; that sorrow and joy mingle together in every bridal cup. For in every sphere of human life

> "Pleasures are like poppies spread;
> You grasp the flower, its bloom is shed,
> Or like the snow-fall in the river—
> A moment white, then melts forever.
> Or like the Borealis' race,
> That flits ere you can point its place;
> Or like the rainbow's lovely form,
> Evanishing amid the storm."

Yes; sorrow is an heir-loom handed down from family to family, through all the generations of mankind. We are *born unto* it as to an entailed inheritance. And it will find its way even into the sacred recess of home; it will invade the sanctity of domestic life, and cloud the brows of the married pair with care. Hence Dr. Fuller has well said to youthful brides and bridegrooms:—

"Deceive not yourselves by over expecting happiness in the married state. Marriage is not like the hill Olympus, wholly clear, without clouds. Remember the nightingales, which sing only some months in the spring, but commonly are silent when they have hatched their eggs, as if their mirth were turned into care for their young ones."

But why utter such dirge-like sounds in the ears of the *newly married?* Why, in these hours, devoted to love and joy, stand before them with words of warning, like the evil genius of Brutus? Why not permit the fond delusions of hope to remain until dispelled by stern reality?

My answer to these questions is, That it is easier to combat a difficulty whose existence and extent are foreknown, than to grapple with it ignorantly and suddenly. Besides, many evils of married life are avoidable. I would, therefore, by these cautions prepare the newly married to meet their necessary trials and sorrows with courage, and instruct them to escape those which are produced rather by errors and follies than by necessity.

CHAPTER II.

On Avoiding the first Quarrel.

THE first quarrel between a man and his wife, like the first glass of wine, is the only dangerous one. Let that be avoided, and that hateful demon, discord, will never find a place at the domestic hearth. Let it have an existence, no matter how trivial the subject, or how brief its duration, the demon will feel himself invited, and will take his place, an odious, but an abiding guest, at the fireside.

Smile not, happy pair, at this caution. You look at each other in the rhapsodies of love, and are ready to say, " *We* shall never quarrel. *Our* love is too deep, too true, too ardent, to wane and die."

Yet love, deep, ardent, true as yours, has been followed by years of bitterness, and even by separation, and all through not avoiding *the first quarrel*.

Very few newly married persons understand each other's tastes and peculiarities. Most courtships afford anything but an opportunity for gaining this knowledge. In general, courtship consists in mutual, though undesigned, deception. Both parties labour to *conceal* their unfavourable points of character: both aim to please, and are determined to be pleased. If the judgment dares to intermeddle with the passions, and to suggest unfitness or uncongeniality, its faithful voice is silenced. One purpose inspires both minds,—they are determined to marry at all events.

Too often, courtship is so brief, so hasty, so artificial, that, if really desirous to judge of their mutual congeniality, the parties have no sufficient opportunity. What is the prevailing method of courtship? The parties meet, perhaps, at church, or at a party. They are mutually pleased. The young man calls at the lady's home. They sit, chat, walk together. Perhaps they follow that worse than heathenish practice of sitting up together a greater part of the night. They *never* see each other in the duties and trials of life, when acting naturally. Everything between them is artificial; done to promote their common object—marriage. This state of things lasts a few months, and the object is gained. The parties are man and wife.

But all is not real yet. The "*honeymoon*" perpetuates the delusions of courtship. But its duration is brief: it passes away. The lover changes to the husband; the bride becomes the wife. In both, the natural dispositions and tastes, the habits, opinions, and views of life, are different. Such is the strict intimacy of married life that these differences will be discovered.

Then the crisis of conjugal happiness or misery is reached. The parties either yield to each other, learn the art of mutual assimilation, and pass life in comparative enjoyment; or they express their differences, quarrel, and begin a career of domestic misery, ending in separation or death.

This danger in the beginning of wedded life is well expressed by JEREMY TAYLOR, who says:—

"Man and wife are equally concerned to avoid all offences of each other at *the beginning* of their conversation. Every little thing can blast an infant blossom, and the breath of the south can shake the little rings of the vine when first they begin to curl like the locks of a new weaned boy: but when by age and consolidation they stiffen into the hardness of a stem, and have, by the warm embraces of the sun, and the kisses of Heaven, brought forth their clusters, they can endure the storms of the north and the loud noises of a tempest, and yet never be broken. So are the early unions of an unfixed marriage, watchful and observant, apt to take alarm at every unkind word. After the hearts of the man and the wife are endeared and hardened by a mutual confidence and experience, longer than artifice or pretence can last, there are a great many remembrances, and some things present, that dash all little unkindnesses in pieces."

This is well and wisely spoken. A trifling disagreement about a trifling matter may destroy a life of enjoyment. And it usually happens that when the married pair do quarrel, the occasion is so despicable they are ashamed to think of it. Yet that silly circumstance, like a drop of ink discolouring a whole vessel of water, often spreads its influence over the whole life. Just as

> "A pebble in the streamlet scant
>   Has turn'd the course of many a river;
> A dew-drop on the baby plant
>   Has warp'd the giant oak forever."

I find an exceedingly painful illustration of these ideas in an English publication, for the truth of which its author pledges his word.

A young couple had passed the first weeks of their marriage at the house of a friend. Having at length occupied their new home, they were taking their first breakfast, when the following scene occurred:—

The young husband was innocently opening a boiled egg in an egg-cup. The bride observed that he **was breaking** the shell at, what *she thought* was, the wrong end. "How strange it looks," she said, "to see you break your egg at the small end, my dear! No one else does so; and it looks so odd."

"O, I think it's quite as good, in fact better, than breaking it at the large end, my love; for when you break the large end, the egg runs over the top," replied the husband.

"But it looks so very odd, when no one else does so," rejoined the wife.

"Well, now, I really do think it is not a nice way that *you* have got of eating an egg. That dipping strips of bread and butter into an egg certainly is not tidy. But I do not object to your doing as you please, if you will let me break my egg at the small end," retorted the husband.

"I am quite sure my way is not so bad

as eating fruit-pie with a knife, as you do, instead of using the fork; and you always eat up the sirup as if you were not accustomed to have such things. You really do not see how very bad it looks, or I am sure you would not do so," added the wife.

"The sirup is made to be eaten with the pie, and why should I send it away in the plate?" asked the husband.

"No well-bred persons clear up their plates as if they were starved," said the bride, with a contemptuous toss of her little head.

"Well, then, I am not a well-bred person," replied the bridegroom, angrily.

"But you must be, if we are to be comfortable together," was the sharp answer of the fastidious lady.

"Well, I must break my egg at the small end, so it does not signify; and I must also eat the sirup."

"Then I will not have either fruit-pies or eggs at the table."

"But I *will* have them," petulantly exclaimed the husband.

"Then I wish I had not been married to you," cried the young wife, bursting into tears.

"And so do I," added the now incensed husband, as he arose and walked out of the room.

This domestic quarrel was followed by others equally trifling in their origin and disgraceful in their character; until the silly couple made themselves so disagreeable to each other that their home became unendurable, and they separated.

Now, I doubt not, the reader is ready to pronounce this quarrel about opening an egg, a foolish affair. It was so; and yet I seriously question if the first quarrel between a newly married pair ever has a much more elevated beginning. Little things do great mischief, and are to be watched with suspicious care.

I repeat my caution. Beware of the *first* quarrel. Whatever dissimilarity of habit, taste, or feeling, you may discover in each other, be resolute in enduring it; be determined to reconcile yourselves to it, or seek its modification by the gentlest attempts of love. Remember that, however unsuited to each other you may be, the irrevocable covenant has been uttered. You are bound to each other for life; and both prudence and duty demand the concealment of your dislikes, and the strongest efforts to conform to each other's tastes. It will be far easier, in case of such dissimilarity, to crucify your feelings and tastes, than to indulge in useless regrets and bitter quarrels. Begin your married life, therefore, by a stern and fixed resolve to avoid the first quarrel.

CHAPTER III.

Of beginning Married Life Religiously.

MARRIAGE is God's institution. It was the Almighty who said, "It is not good for man to be alone." HE also pronounced the nuptial benediction on the first bridal pair. The Lord Jesus has declared its sanctity under the present dispensation of grace. The Holy Spirit, through the pen of an apostle, has said, "Marriage is honourable in all."

The marriage institution having this heavenly authority, it follows that its claims and duties are consistent with the enjoyment of any and every degree of personal religion, otherwise God would be inconsistent with himself. His requirements would be contradictions, and our obligations to him be dissolved.

But although the congeniality of married life with the claims of spiritual religion is an obvious and undeniable fact, yet very many pious persons have felt scruples, and entertained doubts concerning it. Among these, stands the amiable and devoted FLETCHER, who refrained from a married life for many years, on the sole ground that he thought it "*impossible to be as much devoted to God in a married as in a single life.*"

This opinion he afterwards renounced. Perhaps the reason he gave for changing it may be equally satisfactory to others who have similar views; while the *fact*, that he retained his spirituality both at and after his marriage, gives weight to his reasoning. In an address to some religious friends, shortly after his union with Miss Bosanquet, he thus alluded to his long-cherished but mistaken opinion:—

"But this objection," he said, "had been removed by reading, 'Enoch begat sons and daughters. And Enoch walked with God, and was not, for God took him.' I then saw if Enoch, at the head of a family, might walk with God, and be fit for translation, our souls, under the Gospel dispensation, might attain the highest degree of holiness in a similar state, if too great an attachment, leading the soul *from* God, rather than *to* him, did not take place."

This is a conclusive argument, and it was admirably sustained by his eminently spiritual and holy life; and it is an unquestionable fact, that a large proportion of the brightest and holiest names in the Church of Jesus have been married persons.

The newly married pair may therefore rest assured of the possibility of maintaining a spiritual mind through their bridal hours. If they *will* it, Jesus will sit with them at the bridal feast, and consecrate the bridal chamber by his presence. He will smile upon their new home, brighten their happiest hours, and gently lead them through the changeful future, until they sit joyfully down at His marriage supper, when he will be united to his spouse, the Church, in everlasting bonds.

Alas! how seldom do such marriages

occur! Very few Christians pass into this holy state without losing a degree of their piety. Jesus is not cordially invited to the wedding. The bridal chamber is not consecrated by prayer. The carnal triumphs over the spiritual. The Holy Spirit is grieved, and the home of the newly married is not honoured by the presence and blessing of a pure and holy God.

If the blessing of God is of that infinite value which our holy religion teaches it to be, this consequence ought to be avoided. It were better not to marry than to backslide in the act. But it can, and ought to be prevented. Only let the young couple resolve to begin their married life in a strictly religious manner, and all will be well. Let their conversation be spiritual; let the bridal chamber witness their prayers and their covenants to serve Christ together; let the social altar be erected at once, and their hearts cheerfully laid upon it, and Jesus will pronounce a nuptial benediction, which will bring them happiness and prosperity through the years of after life. But

> "Alas for those who love, and cannot blend in prayer!"

Some newly married persons think themselves excused from establishing an altar for social worship because they compose the whole family. "Did my family contain more than myself and my wife, I should think it very proper to establish social worship," is the young husband's excuse. Hence, he begins the organization of his family wrong. And being begun wrong, it is too easy to continue so, when, in the course of nature, his family is increased.

This is sinful. The young couple should consecrate their home to God the first time they occupy it. They should strictly maintain the daily practice of reading the Scriptures and praying together, through life. The presence of visitors, the introduction of boarders or domestics, the increase of the family by children, should not be permitted to overturn the sacred altar. Morning and evening, from the nuptial day to the day of burial, should witness the ascending incense of gratitude, love, and prayer. I assure the reader of this friendly counsel, that, on a death-bed, such an inviolability of the family altar would be a delightful recollection.

The benefits of thus establishing family religion cannot be fully described. They will never be known in their full extent until eternity shall unfold its sweet revealings. Then it will be seen how such devotion softened the asperities of temper, sweetened the spirit, prevented discords, promoted forgiveness, fanned the dim flame of personal religion, aided in family government, impressed domestics and children with the idea of God, of human responsibility, of the necessity of pure religion, and how, above all, it brought down the blessing of Heaven, like dew on Hermon's brow, and called forth from the lips of the Eternal God that commendation on the Christian husband, which, in ancient times, he pronounced on Abraham, "I know him, that he will command his children and his household after him to do justice and judgment." "What a union of two believers," says TERTULLIAN, "to have one hope, one desire, one course of life, one service of God, in common the one with the other! Both, like brother and sister, undivided in heart and flesh, fall down together on their knees, and pray. Christ's peace is on such as these. Where two are, there is He; and where He is, evil cannot come."

Nor is social worship the only religious duty incumbent upon you. It is important that you also begin right in the matter of attending public worship. Covenant together to be punctual in your attendance at the house of God. Be not like wandering stars, roaming from church to church, but select your spiritual home, and resort to it constantly, *from a sense of duty.*

If it be possible, attend at least twice on the Sabbath. To do this, make such arrangements for eating on the Sabbath as

will not trespass on your time or that of
your domestics. Avoid the guilty practice
of many fashionable professors of religion,
who keep their domestics at home in the
morning to cook a luxurious dinner, while
they are at church. They come home,
spend a long time at the table, and then
loll away the afternoon in idleness. This
is a very sinful practice. What right have
such persons to compel their domestics to
break the Sabbath? God bids both servant and master to avoid work on his holy
day. By what right does the master dare
to contravene the authority of God? What
excuse can be offered for wasting the Sabbath afternoon in idleness? Is the Sabbath
kept holy by merely spending an hour in
God's house? O shame! Shame on such
pretended Christians! They have not
taken their first lessons in self-denial, and
can hardly hope to pass the ordeal of that
judgment, which will recognize, as one of
its immutable laws, this saying of the august
Judge, "If a man will come after me, let

him deny himself, and take up his cross, and follow me."

To avoid these evils, let the bridal couple here addressed *begin right*. Adopt it as a rule in your house, that PUBLIC WORSHIP MUST BE ATTENDED THROUGH THE LORD'S DAY, BY ALL THE HEALTHY MEMBERS OF THE FAMILY; and let all other things be arranged to correspond with this paramount Sabbath duty. Do this *now*, and when you are surrounded by the young "*olive plants*," which will grow up around your table, you will not be afflicted, as many parents are, who *cannot* persuade, and *will not* compel, their children to attend the worship of God.

But what shall be said to those two creatures of God who have entered the sacred precincts of marriage without religious feelings? There is something awful and daring in their spirit. They have endeavoured to *isolate themselves from God*. They have acted independently of their Maker, just as they would have done if he had had no existence. O, terrible boldness! Married without God! Without prayer! Without humble dependence on his care! Alas for them in the day of their calamity! Who shall aid them when their neglected God shall permit "his fury to fly up into his face," and come forth in judgment against them?

Such a marriage cannot be fruitful of bliss. It is a tree at whose roots the living waters do not flow; it must, therefore, fail of greenness and fruit in the time of drought: for "marriage is an institution of God, and cannot possibly be enjoyed except in the Spirit of God."

The home of such a marriage will speedily become joyless. It is not sufficiently spiritual to produce lasting bliss; for "an irreligious union is a sensual union, and sensuality is volatile. The many irksome marriages which there are, are miserable, most of them, for the want of an indwelling spiritual sentiment." The parties do not see themselves clothed with immortality, and destined for a spiritual union, long after their earthly forms exist no longer; hence the loftiest and most ennobling aims of life are absent from their intercourse. Life's wheels drag heavily along, "for want of that infinite depth of sentiment of which Christianity is in the human soul the fountain."

"Alas for that home in which the highest theme of the husband's discourse is the last acute bargain which he made in business; or the levity, coarse, perhaps, as well as trifling, which he last heard at the tavern! Alas for that home in which the wife, on opening her heart, discloses no traces of any nobler feelings than such as the larder or the laundry might suggest! Alas for her who establishes no higher claims on her husband's regards than mere fidelity to his person, and frugality and order in his house."—MOUNTFORD.

As, then, you have been married to each other, so let each be married to Christ. Though you have entered on the duties of marriage in an unconsecrated home, let it remain so no longer. By all your hopes of connubial bliss; your anticipations of uninterrupted happiness; by your wishes for eternal life,—I exhort you to embrace the religion of Christ. Kneel side by side, in penitential prayer, until the Everlasting arms embrace you both, and the Eternal voice pronounces a nuptial benediction upon your souls. Then will your conjugal intercourse be purified; your union will be spiritual; your minds, as well as your bodies, will be one. You will have that sympathy, sensibility, patience, faith, love, necessary to the harmony of life; and you will also be enabled to anticipate with delight the reunion of your spirits after death.

How consolatory is this latter prospect to two souls joined in the purest friendship to each other! Its power was sublimely apparent at the martyrdom of SIMON MARECHAL and his wife. As they approached the stake, and beheld the horrid preparations for their burning, she turned to her husband, and, in the true spirit of heroic and Christian love, said,—

"Dear husband, our marriage has hitherto been but an engagement. This is our true wedding-day; when, after this trifling torment, the Son of God will marry us for eternity."

The religion which converted the martyr flame of this devoted pair into a nuptial couch, and inspired their mutual love with more than the freshness of the marriage hour, is for you, beloved ones, who now read these lines. Seek it now, and keep it forever.

CHAPTER IV.

Of Religious Differences.

It is possible these pages may fall into the hands of a youthful pair who belong to churches of a different name. Such a difference in church connexions is an evil in some respects; it may, if due care be not taken, become a root of exceeding bitterness. Yea, it may grow into a deadly upas-tree, beneath whose poisonous shadow, husband, wife, and little ones, may lie down in the darkness of the second death.

But this need not be, if the difficulty be met in the true spirit of sanctified love. Such a spirit will find a method by which to avoid unhappy consequences.

Perhaps the best mode would be for the parties to compromise the matter. *If no question of conscience* is involved, one of the parties might join the church of the other. Still neither should insist upon this. The right to worship God conscientiously is too sacred to be invaded by either husband or wife; but if either party could, *with a satisfied conscience*, and for the glory of God, relinquish past preferences, it would be a happy consummation. If this cannot be, then the evil must be submitted to in the spirit of true affection. Each must worship at the chosen altar, occasionally visiting each other's church, and carefully avoiding all reproach, and all manifestations of sectarian bigotry. Let each remember that they stood at the altar with the foresight of this difference; and that the conjugal vow binds them to respect each other's preferences, and to yield to each other the sacred rights of conscience. The same liberal and Christian feeling must influence them, when they become parents, in the education of their children, though, in this matter, the wife is bound to remember that the husband is the divinely appointed *head* of the family. The right and the authority to decide in their case, are unquestionably in his hands, to be exercised, however, with all mildness and discretion, and in the fear of God.

But possibly these greetings and counsels may be read by a couple, one of whom is a child of God, and the other a stranger to spiritual things. The Christian and the sinner stand joined together in holy bonds; and, however closely they may be united in affection, there is a great religious gulf between them.

The difficulty to be overcome in such a case is a very serious one. It is the more so, because a great fault lies at its foundation. The Christian *ought* to have married *only in the Lord*, that is, with another Christian, and is, therefore, weakened and unfitted for successful conflict by the want of a good conscience toward God. Still, the evil may not be without its remedy, and must, at least, be *endured*.

I think the first duty of the Christian, in such a case, is to be humbled before God. A forbidden union has been formed. A friend of Christ has joined hands and heart with an enemy of God. But the union is irrevocable. The die is cast. The sacred seal of marriage is upon the parties, and it cannot be broken. But the spirit, the carnal spirit, which led you, child of God, to give your affections to an unrenewed person, can and must be mourned over before God, until you are assured of forgiveness and peace.

This done, the kiss of peace from Mercy's lips having sealed your pardon, you must dedicate yourself to an unwearied effort to bring your partner to Christ. Assume it as a settled question, that you must either convert your partner or be yourself lured into a sinful life. True, the maintenance of your present moral state is barely possible; but it is a fact of rare experience that a saint and sinner joined in marriage bonds retain their respective characters until death. No; the saint either wins the sinner to Christ, or apostatizes under the carnal influence of the Christless companion. Of you, my dear reader, I hope better things, and therefore exhort you to make it YOUR CHIEF WORK TO CONVERT YOUR COMPANION TO CHRIST.

To succeed in this Divine work, you must commence it in a proper manner. And what is more proper than simplicity and frankness on the subject? Much is often lost in religious effort through a want of a full and free explanation between the parties. Opposition springs up, when a soul might be saved if approached in a proper manner.

I will suppose a case, by way of illustrating what I think is the most likely method of commencing an effort for the salvation of a husband or wife.

A young lady, I will call her MISS EMILY CHURCHILL, is soundly converted to Christ. Her experience is so clear, her testimony so emphatic, her spirit so sweet and humble, that none doubt the reality of the gracious work. She is one of those Christians who can say, with the sacred poet,—

"Not a cloud doth arise,
To darken the skies,
Or hide for one moment
My Lord from my eyes."

This heavenly frame is maintained for several months, when a young gentleman, I will call him MR. THEODORE HUME, attracted by her simple, intellectual beauty, begins to pay her some especial attentions. Mr. Hume is respectable, moral, educated, the son of pious parents, an attendant at the house of God, but an unconverted man. He treats religion with cold respect, yet feels towards it that deep-rooted aversion which characterizes every man who is "without God and without hope in the world." Still, he is attracted to Miss Churchill by her many estimable qualities; and though he would prefer a lady less puritanic and less strict, yet he resolves to woo and to wed her if possible.

Emily, flattered by the attentions of so amiable a young gentleman, admits him freely to her home. Gradually her interest in him increases, until, before she is hardly conscious of the fact, the spell of love is on her heart. Mr. Hume, emboldened by her obvious regard for him, proposes marriage.

Emily is embarrassed, and prudently asks time to consider so weighty a question. A conflict ensues, in which her clear religious duty "to marry only in the Lord," contends mightily with her inclination to unite her fortunes with those of her beloved Theodore. She carries the matter to a throne of grace for direction; but her heart, already captivated by her lover, is disinclined to really submit the question to God, and, consequently, her prayers effect nothing. Still, she battles with her convictions, and by a process of self-deception, but too well understood by those who study themselves, she persuades herself that *she* may violate the plain will of God concerning the marriage of believers, and be guiltless, because, forsooth, she hopes Mr. Theodore Hume may in some time to come be a child of God.

They stand at the altar, a lovely pair, "the admired of all admirers." The bridal weeks pass rapidly away. The novelty of her new state is gone. The romantic visions of courtship have given place to the sober realities of wedded life, with all its variety of pleasure and pain, of joy and sorrow, of hopes and fears.

Emily has been the subject of painful misgivings since the hour in which she decided to accept Mr. Hume as her betrothed; and they have borne their baleful fruit in her heart. Her religious affections have received a check; her zeal for God has diminished; her faith has weakened: and from being an eminently devoted disciple, she has sunk down to the level of the ordinary and powerless professor. And notwithstanding she has taken her place in the temple of marriage, and is the mistress of a beautiful home, she cannot refrain from a frequent and sorrowful gaze at the past : a gaze which extorts the cry of,—

"What peaceful hours I once enjoy'd;
 How sweet their mem'ry still!
But they have left an aching void
 The world can never fill."

While she is in this state of mind, her pastor preaches a pungent discourse on backsliding in heart. The arrow, sharp with pointed truth, enters her soul. The religious principle revives in the might of its Divine power: she mourns over her error; and, soliciting forgiveness from God, resolves to do what may yet be done to atone for it, by seeking to win her husband to Christ.

This is all she can now do. Wishes to escape from the marriage bond would be both wrong and useless. That bond is indissoluble, except by the hand of death. Emily understands this, and hence she fixes her attention on the sole remedy— the conversion of her husband. She begins the work by a conversation, something like the following:—

It is Sabbath evening. They have just

returned from church, where they have listened to a very solemn discourse; and are seated together in their snug little parlour. Having prepared herself by previous prayer, Emily tremblingly begins her important work by remarking, "We have heard a very weighty sermon to-night."

"Yes, if all is true that the preacher said, it was weighty enough to produce some effect; but that is the great question. Are these things all true?"

Emily wisely evades the controversy about the truth of the Gospel, which her husband seems willing to provoke, and replies, "The truth of the Gospel is written on our own hearts. We sin, and guilt disturbs our peace. We instinctively shrink from the future, and tremble to stand unmasked before God. Whereas, if we obtain the forgiveness of those sins by faith in Jesus Christ, instead of dreading, we desire to meet, the Judge of all."

This appeal to experience reminds the young husband that his wife is a professor of the Christian faith, and he inquires, "Do you think, Emily, that a person may **really** know his sins forgiven?"

"Do I *think* it? Yes, my husband, and I *know* it, too, by my own sweet experience," the young wife replies, her soul kindling with holy ardour, as she thus boldly bears witness to the truth of Christ.

"You seem very confident, Emily," responds Mr. Hume, with a dryness of manner which is designed to cool the fervour of his wife.

"Yes, I *am* confident, because the power of grace on my spirit has been too manifest to be denied. It is too true, however, that for several months I have lived without a clear consciousness of the favour of Christ. But recently the favour of God has been restored to me, and my joy would be complete but for one fact."

"What is that one fact, Emily?" asks Mr. Hume.

"I almost tremble to utter it," she replies, as the tears fill her expressive eyes; "but I know my husband will not be angry. I am filled with concern, my dear husband, for the safety of your soul. I see you living in an unrenewed state. I know if you die thus, we shall be eternally separated; and that thought is distressing to me, beyond my power to express it."

Mr. Hume is moved, as any husband would be under similar circumstances; but it is not in human nature to yield to a single attack of truth; so, coughing to clear his voice, he responds, with affected indifference, "I am doing well enough, Emily. I think you need not be troubled on my account."

"O say not so, my husband. Your soul is in danger. I cannot rest to see it thus exposed. How can I, as your wife, view the possibility of our endless separation in another life? Do, my dear husband, do let me persuade you to yield yourself to God, and become a Christian. Do let us travel together to the same place, that we may make our union eternal."

The husband's feelings are touched still more deeply by this appeal. He feels a movement of submission to God in his soul. But, in the same instant, the pride of his heart takes fire; the natural aversion of his nature to the holy God rises into life; and, suppressing his emotions, he responds, "Why, Emily, from whence does this new-born zeal for me spring forth so suddenly? We have been intimate for two years, and married several months, yet, until now, you have never shown the existence of such emotions. I do not understand this; neither do I feel like being dragged into a religious life by the force of feeling."

Emily perceives the ascendency of the carnal nature in her husband, and meekly explains to him the manner of her backsliding, and of her restoration to Divine favour. Here the conversation rests for the present. A beginning has been made. The husband fully understands her feelings; and, though hating religion, cannot be really angry with his Emily; for her humble meekness and devoted love disarm wrath even in his unrenewed mind.

I would like to close this imaginary dialogue by supposing the speedy success of Emily; but this I cannot do without violating the truth of human experience. Speedy conversions, in such marriages, though possible, and of occasional occurrence, are rare. Those Christians who marry out of Christ usually see their companions remain a long time in the same state, though the length of the period depends, after a proper commencement of direct effort, on the consistency of the Christian's life. Let that be exemplary; let the direct effort be prudently continued, and accompanied by fervent prayer, and an early conquest may be hoped for.

This parabolic story needs no comment; it carries its own instruction to the reader, who has done as Emily did. I trust the high purpose and holy effort of our imaginary heroine may find an incarnation and an actual existence in the experience of such readers.

That the religious party in one of these sinful marriages may not wholly despair of leading the other party into the delightful captivity of the Gospel of Jesus, I will relate a fact, which I find in a recent publication:*—

"A gentleman," says this writer, "with whom I am personally acquainted, had for many years no love for religion, no respect for Christian profession. He married a lady who was a professed Christian; but they agreed that, on the subject of religion, they would disagree. He was not to trouble her, or in any way interfere with her religious privileges or faith. She was not to trouble him on the subject of his soul's salvation. Some years after his marriage he became interested upon religion, and was a hopeful convert to God. He felt, as every child of God will feel, that he ought

* "Counsels to Married Persons," by Rev. M. H. Smith.

to erect a family altar, and gather his household around it, for service, morning and evening. It was a solemn occasion. The husband, once stout-hearted and rebellious, was now penitent and subdued—the wife was weeping for joy at the mercy of God which had visited her house, and at the answer which at length had been given to prayer long continued—and the children wondered at the strange sight.

"All were together. As the husband and father took in his hand the holy book of God, he turned to his wife, and said,—

"'I cannot begin this solemn service, and erect an altar here, without first acknowledging how much I am indebted to you as an instrument, in the hands of God, of my conversion. On the day of my marriage I had no confidence in religion. I was a mocker at the truths of God. I said, my wife professes to be a Christian. I will see in her conduct what religion is; I will know if there is any reality in the Christian profession. From that moment I have had my eye upon you. I have watched you in every position in which you have been placed. I have seen you in moments of joy and grief; in your relations to the family and to the Church; in those hours of relaxation in which the mind is unbent; in those seasons of communion with your Saviour, when, with a firm voice and fervent spirit, you have prayed for my salvation; and when you knew not that my ear heard your petition. I have seen your joy, as you have clasped the new-born babe to your bosom; and I have witnessed your anguish as you have laid that babe in the silent grave. I became satisfied that your religion was real; that you were actuated by a principle that I did not possess; that you were sustained by a power to which I was a stranger. To your holy walk, consistent life, and godly conversation, I owe my salvation.'

"Tears of gratitude choked his utterance: his wife, no longer able to control her feelings, burst out in loud sobs and cries; the children blended their small voices with the voice of their parents. All fell on their knees, and thus erected their first family altar."

This was certainly a happy issue; but the risk was fearful, and the trial severe to that struggling wife before the hour of triumph came. Let her success, however, encourage others who may have fallen into a similar lot, to consistently labour for the salvation of their unconverted partners.

But I cannot pass from this question without a brief appeal to the unconverted husband or wife who has married a Christian companion. I do this the more earnestly, because many such have become SORE PERSECUTORS of their Christian partners; embittering their married life for no other cause than their devotion to Christ. Perhaps a few pictures, roughly sketched from real life, may best exhibit the WICKEDNESS, the CONTEMPTIBLE MEANNESS, and THE UNNATURAL VILENESS OF SUCH DOMESTIC PERSECUTORS.

A young man, whom I will designate ROBERT WILLIS, a citizen of ——, owing either to a want of a proper understanding of Christian duty, or to a wilful affection, married an unconverted young lady. As is usual in such cases, his heart was in a state of spiritual defection, and, consequently, he did not attempt the erection of a family altar at the time of his marriage. Some months more of religious delinquency followed, when, his soul being quickened, he proposed to begin the long-neglected duty of family prayer.

"No," said his wife; "I want no praying. We have got along without it thus far, and I don't wish to begin it now."

"But I feel it to be a solemn duty I owe to God, and I must perform it or lose the favour of God."

"You have obtained some new light, I suppose. Why did you not do so before?"

Poor Mr. Willis sighed deeply at this unkind question. It was a dart thrust into a sore place; but repressing his feelings, he replied, "Maria, you know I have been backslidden for a long time. I have neglected many religious duties; but am now resolved, by the help of God, to devote my best efforts to him and to his cause."

"Well, do as you please; but I don't want any praying where I am," answered his wicked wife.

But Mr. Willis was firm, and asserted his unquestionable right as a husband to establish an altar for God. The first time, his wife contemptuously sat playing with the leaves of a book while he was in prayer. The next, she noisily left the room; and scarcely a day passed in which she did not invent some petty annoyance to discourage her now unhappy husband. At length her opposition became intolerable. She reproached him with bitter names, threw water upon him as he knelt in prayer, and at last dragged him to the floor while he was in the act of pleading with God.

The poor man was subdued. Contend with her, he would not; to persevere against such a fierce, unwomanly spirit, he dared not; and yielding to what he considered the force of circumstances, he ceased to pray: his spirit was humbled and mortified; his domestic peace blasted forever. He is now

> "An old man, hoary white with eld;"

and she is an old woman: but both are unhappy. She will probably die in her sins; and he, if he reach heaven at all, will be saved so as by fire.

This painting is substantially true: its originals move within the sphere of my knowledge: and while my unknown readers contemplate the fiendlike conduct of Maria, let them solemnly vow never to acquire the character of religious persecutors, especially in domestic life. The sword of the persecutor always inflicts two wounds at one blow. His victim suffers by it; but he suffers also. If, then, irreligious husband or wife, you have a pious partner, beware how you begin to persecute or oppose.

The peace of your home, to say nothing of your obligations to God, requires you to give free scope to the religious obligations of your pious partner.

I have known some irreligious husbands to forbid their Christian wives to support the Gospel; to refuse to hire seats for them at church; to scold them if they were not home from meeting precisely at nine o'clock. Others I have known who hindered them from going to meeting by pretending they felt neglected and slighted by their absence. And I knew one man, who actually forbade his wife's pastor from calling at his house. Such acts as these are unmanly: and if their perpetrators knew the estimate formed of their characters by the public, they would refrain for very shame's sake.

These counsels to the *bridal* pair may appear strange and ill-timed. With them it is the hour of love. They are not yet fairly out on the sea of domestic life. Their gay bark is as yet only floating, with streamers flying, on the smooth surface of the matrimonial harbour. It is well, therefore, for them to look out into the sea, whose waters they must cross: and this is the more needful, because they have their choice between the stormy Atlantic of domestic discord, and the quiet placid Pacific of family harmony. A view of the former should have the effect of saving them from venturing on its boisterous bosom. Let Tasso's pilot teach them a valuable lesson:

> "The pilot, who, from the capricious wind,
> O'er seas where quicksands lurk and breakers roar,
> Has steer'd his vessel to the port assign'd,
> Should gather in his canvass, heave ashore,
> Nor trust the traitor winds and cruel ocean more."

Thus, warning should have the effect of experience. Let the irreligious bride or bridegroom learn from the sorrows of others that the best course is to unite with the pious companion, and live together in the embraces of a chaste affection, sanctified by a fervent piety. Such a life is the nearest to the life of heaven permitted to mortals.

CHAPTER V.

Of Relatives and Friends.

"Every beginning is shrouded in a mist," says the poet; and he adds, "The traveller setteth out on his journey oppressed with many thoughts." The experience of the newly married will soon prove the truth of the poet's utterances, for new dangers will start at every advancing step, and the future will often look cloudy to the anxious eye.

A happy domestic life should be regarded as a prize worth having, even at the cost of many struggles. Nor can it be reached without high purposes and decided efforts. Still, if you both determine to enjoy it, it will unquestionably be yours.

In becoming man and wife, you have not only changed your relation to each other, but to your respective families. Both have been admitted into a new family, and very much of your conjugal happiness depends on the union of your families now brought into intimate connexion by your marriage. A delightful harmony, a troublesome jealousy, or a painful indifference will shortly spring up to bless or to trouble you. By proper caution on both sides, an harmonious union, which will make sweet music, may be permanently established.

Should there be a step-mother or a maiden sister who has previously acted as house-keeper for the bridegroom, the young wife may have a task to perform which will demand the employment of all her energies.

In such a case, it is the duty of the husband to transfer, fully and formally, all domestic management from his mother or sister to his wife. There cannot be two mistresses in one domestic establishment; and it is the *right* of the wife to preside as a queen over her own household. Any attempt to divide authority between her and another will certainly create trouble; while no sensible mother or sister will complain, if, at the kind wish of the son or brother, she is requested to defer to the lawful mistress of his home; though very much depends on the gentleness and kindness with which the bride exercises that authority. She should do it with all that love and respect which becomes a daughter or sister-in-law.

A melancholy example of the impropriety of continuing the authority of a mother-in-law in a household, after the introduction of a wife, is furnished in the experience of the celebrated MADAME GUION. It is probable that cases exactly similar are of rare occurrence; yet the young husband, whose mother will continue to be an inmate of his dwelling, may be benefited by a glance at this feature in Madame Guion's history. She describes her bridal reception in her husband's home in the following language:—

"No sooner was I at the house of my husband, than I perceived it would be for me *a house of mourning*. In my father's house every attention had been paid to my manners. I had been encouraged to speak freely on the various questions which were started in our family circle. There, everything was set off in full view; everything was characterized by elegance. But it was very different in the house of my husband, which was chiefly under the direction of his mother, who had long been a widow, and who regarded nothing else but saving. The elegance of my father's house they sneered at as pride. If I had occasion to speak, I was listened to only to be contradicted and reproved. If I spoke well, they said I was endeavouring to give them a lesson in good speaking. If I uttered my opinions on any subject of discussion which came up, I was charged with desiring to enter into a dispute; and instead of being applauded, I was simply told to hold my tongue, and was scolded from morning till night."—*Abridged from Professor Upham's Life of Madame Guion.*

How suddenly must this treatment have extinguished the bright hopes of love in this young bride's heart! It was even so. Sorrow became her portion. Her hymeneal star set in the black clouds of domestic misery. The sweet waters of love turned to wormwood in the marriage cup. She has left a picture, drawn by her own pencil, of the state to which this treatment reduced her. She says:—

"My condition was every way deplorable. My step-mother secured her object. My proud spirit broke under her system of coercion. Married to a person of rank, I found myself a slave in my own dwelling. The treatment which I received so impaired the vivacity of my nature, that I became dumb, like 'the lamb that is shearing.' Terror took possession of my mind. I lost all power of resistance. Under the rod of my despotic mistress I sat dumb, and almost idiotic. Those who had heard of me, but had never seen me before, said one to another, 'Is this the person who sits thus silent like a piece of statuary, that was famed for such an abundance of wit?' In this situation I found no one ... who might share my grief, and help me to bear it. To have made known my feelings and trials to my parents, would only have occasioned new crosses. I was alone and helpless in my grief."—*Upham's Life of Madame Guion.*

The husband who could suffer so beautiful and amiable a woman as Madame Guion to be crushed in the dust by the tyrannical foot of his imperious mother, can hardly escape our contempt. While towards the mother herself we can but feel unmixed disgust. The mere exhibition of such an odious family picture is sufficient to inspire either son or mother with an immutable resolution never to copy the unpardonable silence of Monsieur Guion, or to resemble his cruel, heartless mother.

Where there are no relatives of either husband or wife resident in the newly formed home, caution is still requisite to bring all portions of the two families into permanent harmony. Nothing good is obtained by accident; and this very desirable object can be attained only by fixed purposes and determined effort. But the means are simple and easy. Only let the young husband and wife refrain from all acts and expressions which imply contempt of each other's relations, and then let them manifest a kind, courteous, affectionate spirit, and all will be well. The families of each will acquire regard and respect for each other, their means of social enjoyment be thereby enlarged, and the blessings of all parties descend on the heads of the happy pair, by whose union they have become interested in each other. Constant family correspondence is one link in that golden chain of friendship which should bind those families together who have become connected by intermarriages, and should on no account be neglected.

Every bride and bridegroom have old friends, whose influence will still affect their enjoyment. How to make that influence blessed is also a question worthy of brief consideration.

I can best convey my meaning on one point concerning old friends by sketching an ideal picture, promising the reader, however, that in this sketch I shall be true to the reality of many experiences.

I will name my heroine HENRIETTA. She was a fair, gay maiden, with many suitors. But as she was no coquette, she gave especial encouragement to none until young HENRY BURGESS won her affections. To him she surrendered her heart, and to him she seriously promised her hand. Henry and Henrietta were therefore considered by the friends of both as destined for each other.

But Henry had a fickle mind. While he remained near his chosen one he was faithful to his pledges; but the providence of God removed him to a distant city. At first, his letters were frequent and satisfactory; but they soon became few and far between, and finally ceased altogether.

At length Henrietta was informed that **he** was engaged to another.

She was grieved, wounded, hurt. But being a girl of strong mind, she gradually rose above the trial, and, after a long period, consented to receive the attentions of another, whom in due time she wedded.

It happened some months subsequent to her marriage that her former suitor, Henry, returned to settle in his native town. He was still a single man, having been as fickle to his lady abroad as he had been to Henrietta at home. Such were the habits of the place, that they could not avoid meeting each other occasionally; and, as Henrietta was of a forgiving spirit, his apologies for his infidelity to his purposes were accepted, and he was invited by Henrietta and her husband to call.

He did so. Henrietta still felt a strong regard for him, notwithstanding his unfaithfulness, and was rather pleased than otherwise with his frequent visits. By degrees he grew quite familiar, until Henrietta's husband began to be troubled with feelings of jealousy—feelings, it must be admitted, which were quite natural under such circumstances.

One evening her husband very kindly said, "I do not like to see Mr. Burgess so frequently at our house."

The young wife blushed slightly, and replied, "Why, what harm can there be in his friendly visits, Edwin?"

"Perhaps there is none; but I should be better pleased if his visits were more formal and not so frequent."

"But, Edwin, what can be your objections to Mr. Burgess?"

"I have no special objections; but I wish you to discourage his visits."

"Would you have me act uncivilly towards him?"

"By no means. Merely let him understand that his relations to us, while they are friendly, must not be familiar."

"You talk strangely, Edwin. I hope you are not jealous."

"No, Henrietta, I am not jealous; but such were Mr. Burgess's relations to you before our marriage, that I consider his present familiarity highly improper, and shall expect you to discourage it."

Henrietta looked slightly indignant; but biting her lips, she repressed her anger, and was silent. A breach was made in their peace, which grew wider and wider, resulting at last in bitter quarrels, mutual reproaches, and permanent misery.

The reader is, without doubt, prepared to pass a sentence of imprudence upon Henrietta. She deserves it; and if the bride or bridegroom who studies her picture, and has had similar connexions, will learn the lesson, that OLD FRIENDS OF THE OPPOSITE SEXES FOR WHOM STRONG ATTACHMENTS HAVE BEEN FORMED ARE NOT NOW TO BE RECEIVED AS INTIMATE FRIENDS, I shall not have drawn my sketch in vain. For a wife to receive marked attentions from a previous suitor, or a husband to exhibit a peculiar interest in a lady he formerly wooed, is not only obviously improper, but will be a sure cause of jealousy, disagreement, and misery. *Such old friendships are not, therefore, to be cultivated.*

It is also possible that some individuals among your old friends may be disagreeable to one of you. Some female friend of the bride may be unwelcome to the husband, or some male friend of the husband an object of prejudice to the bride. In either case, it is best to discontinue such intimacies, especially if the dislike has a plausible occasion in the character, habits, or manners of the parties. The choice lies between the loss of an old associate or of conjugal unity; and in such a case there is no room for a moment's hesitation. Nevertheless, it would be wise in both to yield to each other's preferences and friendships as far as possible.

In your new relation to each other you will find it necessary to form some new friendships; but it is not wise to form many *intimate* friendships. While every Christian's bosom heaves with good-will towards all, his confidence can be given to very few. To married persons, especially, *confidants* are unnecessary; they can, and ought to confide in each other. The writer of "Proverbial Philosophy" (M. F. Tupper) speaks thus strongly. He says:—

"Let no one have thy confidence, O wife, saving thine husband:
Have not a friend more intimate, O husband, than thy wife."

This is good counsel. Probably no one cause has disturbed the harmony of domestic intercourse more than the imprudent admission of others to the confidence of man or wife. The wife has poured out the griefs of her heart, described the faults of her husband, and vented her spleen at certain unsatisfactory arrangements in her home or circumstances to some female friend. That friend, perhaps thoughtlessly, through a mere intention to sympathize, has fallen in with the opinions of the complaining wife; has persuaded her that she has great hardships to endure, and even intimated the propriety of resistance. Thus musing, in a wrong direction, upon her little griefs, the young wife's trials have magnified themselves from real molehills into ideal mountains. Her spirit has contracted sourness and discontent; her affections have cooled toward her husband; confidence between them has ceased, and their lives have passed away unhappily: and all this through the influence of an injudicious friend.

Young reader, let me implore *you* to avoid this ruinous catastrophe. Have friends, few, select, worthy; but have only one *confidant*—the partner of your bosom. Only let a perfect confidence exist between yourselves, and your hearts will not sigh for the intruding counsels of others. Hear our philosophizing poet once more:—

"If thou wilt be loved, render implicit confidence:
If thou wouldst not suspect, receive full confidence in turn:

> For where trust is not reciprocal, the love that
> trusted withereth.
> Hide not your grief nor your gladness; be open one
> with the other;
> Let bitterness be strange unto your tongues; but
> sympathy a dweller in your hearts.
> Imparting halveth the evils, while it doubleth the
> pleasures of life;
> But sorrows breed and thicken in the gloomy bosom
> of reserve."—TUPPER.

I once knew a married lady, virtuous, affectionate, and pious, into whose family a young gentleman of respectable character and insinuating manners was introduced for a few days. The lady's husband was very properly accustomed to call his wife by her name, Emma. The gentleman visitor, hitherto a stranger, had not been domiciled with them more than two days before he also began to speak to the lady by the name of Emma. And the husband had to endure the mortification of hearing his wife hourly addressed after the following manner by one who was almost a stranger: "Emma, will you take a walk this afternoon?" or, "Emma, how do you like this author?" or, "Emma, I will thank you for another cup of tea."

The lady received this familiar address with evident pleasure. It was innocently offered, and as purely received. But what bride cannot see the imprudency of that wife? Learn, then, young bride and bridegroom, that even innocent familiarities are not to be allowed between you and persons of opposite sexes. Compel all who enter your habitation to observe the strictest proprieties of Christian intercourse, by maintaining a becomingly dignified deportment, and discouraging the first approaches toward their violation. A contrary course has entailed jealousy and ruin on the parties times without number.

CHAPTER VI.
Home and its Arrangements.

YOUR relation of man and wife occasions a necessity hitherto unfelt. You need a *home* which you may call *your own*, and in which you will be the sovereigns. Hitherto you have been dwellers in the home of your parents; now you, in your turn, must create a home for yourselves. The character of that home depends entirely upon yourselves. You may be rich, and some proud mansion, with its soft carpets and stately rooms, may await your occupation; or you may be poor, and some humble cot, with its simple furniture, may be your lot. Which of these two extremes is yours, matters but little; indeed, the outward appearance has very little to do with the character of the home you are about to form. It is in your power to create a domestic heaven in the lowliest cottage; you can suffer the torments of a social hell in the most princely dwelling. Whether, therefore, your sphere be that of merchant princes, of the sturdy tillers of the soil, the laborious artisans, the toilers in professional life, or of those whose only capital and skill lie in their strength of muscle and their will to labour, you should make an immutable purpose to create a *happy* home,—a home like that of Montgomery's shepherd,—

"The fairy ring of bliss"

As the power to do so lies within yourselves, be resolute to call it forth. Your *will*, more potent than Aladdin's lamp, can call into existence, if not the most splendid, at least the most happy home on earth.

But to do this some prudent forethought is necessary. Mountains, you know, are composed of atoms, and oceans of tiny drops. These are so essential, that if the atoms and drops be taken away, the mountains and oceans disappear. It is even so with a happy home. If certain little practical things are lacking in its formation, it will soon cease to be the abode of bliss.

It would be great folly, even for a bird, if a pair of newly mated swallows should build an *eagle's* nest on the summit of a tall mountain crag for their home. Perhaps the world contains no pair of swallows sufficiently unwise to build such a nest. No; the little creatures, taught by their divine instincts, prefer the lowlier shelter of house or barn. It would have been well for many a human pair had they taken lessons in prudence from the birds, as the following etching from real life will prove:—

Mr. Stephen Hale and Miss Maria Adams became man and wife. They spent their honey-moon with their friends, and, after some six or eight weeks, made preparations to create a home for themselves. Mr. Hale was a retail merchant, doing a business which gave him an income of about six hundred dollars. His bride brought him a small sum, perhaps three hundred dollars; all his capital was invested in his business, and could not be safely withdrawn.

Their first attempt was to hire a suitable tenement. They proceeded, in company, to examine the various habitations which were "to let." Several were rejected as too small, too large, or inconvenient. At last they found two adapted to their necessities.

"Well, Maria, which shall I hire?" asked Mr. Hale on their return home.

"I prefer the one on B—— street; it is in the most genteel street, and is more fashionably finished. The paper in the parlour is very beautiful," replies the young wife.

"Yes, that is all true, Maria; and I prefer that house as a matter of taste; but since the other, in D—— street, is well situated, very convenient, and twenty-five dollars per annum less rent, I am inclined to engage it as a matter of economy."

"O, I hope you won't, Stephen. Twenty-five dollars on a year's rent is not much. The house in B—— street is so genteelly finished, and will look so beautiful when it is furnished; I do hope you will take my choice."

"But, Maria, had we not better study economy? One hundred and seventy dollars a year is a very high rent for me to pay in my circumstances. I can manage pretty well to pay one hundred and forty-five, though that is high for my resources."

"I know it is rather high for us to pay; but do let us take it for one year, and we will try to economize in some other way."

When could a fond young husband resist the pleadings of a coaxing bride? The reader already anticipates the result. Maria is successful. The house in B—— street is hired.

This done, they proceed to select their furniture. It has been agreed between them that to enable Mr. Hale to proceed unembarrassed in his business, Maria's three hundred dollars should be expended on furniture. With ordinary prudence in the purchases, this sum would prove amply sufficient.

But their house is in a *genteel* neighbourhood, and must be *genteelly* furnished. They must have at least one room fit to receive company. The carpet, therefore, must be Brussels; the tables of the newest fashion; the chairs mahogany: they must have a set of candelabras, an astral, and a fine sofa. Thus pleaded Maria; the husband yielded, though with some misgivings, and when they had selected their parlour furniture one-half of Maria's money was expended.

Still, the idea of gentility prevailed. They went on purchasing, until, when all was obtained, and the bills came in, Mr. Hale found himself obliged to draw upon his business resources for one hundred dollars.

"Never mind, Stephen: if I had not had my three hundred dollars it would have cost you much more, you know. And see how nice our rooms appear! Isn't this parlour *genteel?* And our sitting-room is almost good enough for a parlour. Now tell me, don't you think everything is in beautiful order?"

Mr. Hale is, of course, silenced, if not convinced, by these bridal persuasives. They are now fairly out on the fickle sea of domestic life. For a time the wind seems favourable, the waters are tolerably smooth, and the sky clear. After a few months, however, a cloud lowers. Maria must keep a servant. Stephen is willing, but fears he cannot meet the additional expense. His business still feels the loss of that hundred dollars expended for furniture, and the rent makes a heavy draught on his income. Still, there is no alternative. Maria's health is growing delicate, and a servant is added to the family.

The first year of their married life is gone. A fine little boy is in the arms of Mr. Hale, who feels a manly pride as he beholds this new treasure. The sickness of Maria, and her unwillingness to leave so *genteel* a neighbourhood, prevents them from moving, and the house in B—— street is hired for another year.

Expenses continue to increase in the little family, until, at the expiration of the second year, Mr. Hale ascertains that he has exceeded his income, and is going behind. He pleads with Maria to move into a cheaper house; but her pleadings are still successful. The house in B—— street is engaged the third year.

That third year has not expired ere Mr. Stephen Hale is insolvent. He settles as he can with his creditors, and, much mortified, removes his residence to a much cheaper and really inferior house. He is a discouraged man, and henceforth *struggles* to find a maintenance for his growing family; whereas, by prudent economy in the commencement, he might have lived without embarrassment.

There are thousands of families situated

as we have just left Mr. and Mrs. Hale, who begin their married life under equally favourable auspices, and who, by prudent arrangements, might have lived out all their days in pecuniary comfort. They have learned the truth of Poor Richard's proverb: "Pride breakfasted with plenty, dined with poverty, and supped with infamy."

If the bridal pair, into whose hands these pages may fall, will follow the few simple rules which I am about to give, they will almost infallibly escape the fate of Maria and her husband.

And, first of all, there should be a frank and full explanation of your pecuniary resources. The husband must let his wife know precisely what his means are. You must then agree together to keep your expenditures *within* your income. They must not be on a scale of equality with it, because you are liable to a variety of casual expenses which can be met only by having some surplus resources. Adopt this, therefore, as an imperative rule, "WE WILL LIVE WITHIN OUR INCOME."

This is easily said, but not so easily done; especially if your income is barely sufficient for comfortable support. Much decision, self-denial, and economical skill, will be requisite to carry your resolution into practice. You must regulate the rent of your dwelling, the character of your diet, the costliness of your clothing, and especially your *little expenses*, by this rule. The habits of others, and even their remarks on your mode of living, must exert no influence over your purpose. The peace and happiness of your entire life depend, in a very high degree, upon the habits of expenditure formed during the first years of your married life.

To carry out this principle with success, you will find it necessary to keep an exact *account* of your expenditures. A little book can be easily procured for this purpose. By this means you can tell at a glance the precise state of your affairs. It will also serve as a powerful check on your *small expenses.* The little sums paid out for ices, confectionary, pastry, cigars, perfumeries, soda water, and various other useless, not to say injurious luxuries, by many small families, form the unseen leak which is sinking them to ruin. A rigid account of daily expenses, faithfully kept, will enable you to see the actual cost of these "*little expenses,*" and thereby lead you to save for real necessities and benevolent purposes.

There should also be some prudent calculations concerning the future. Some small resources should be provided for the "rainy days" of life and for old age, if God should spare you to see them. I have sometimes doubted whether a Christian was bound to lay up property for future contingencies: but my doubts have passed away. Those scriptures which forbid us to lay up treasures on earth, refer to that covetous spirit which converts perishable gold into a deity, and makes property peculiarly the *treasure* of the soul. Such a spirit I deprecate. I warn you against it as you value your salvation. It is not to the accumulation of *riches* I urge you, but merely to provide for casualties and conditions to which you are liable.

God has given us a variety in the seasons of the year. By this arrangement the earth is fruitful only at a given period. By that fact He teaches us the duty of laying by a store of food in summer to meet the demands of our nature during the winter. Should we, through wilful prodigality, refuse to co-operate with this manifest law of nature, and waste the summer fruits in extravagant self-indulgence, we could hope for nothing but suffering in winter. Is it not equally so with the periods and laws of life? Life has its seasons. Its infancy is the season of dependence; its youth, of preparation; its manhood, of action and production; its age, of rest and dependence. God has provided natural protectors for the first season of dependency; the parent is the provider for the infant: but for the last he has made none, unless it be said the child should then provide for the parent. True, he should, rather than see his parent suffer; but he has his own burdens to bear; his own provision to collect; his own children to maintain. Every parent, therefore, should, if it be possible, make provision to meet the wants of the final period of life, without being dependent on his children.

If these views are correct, the new married pair should begin their household arrangements so as to meet this necessity, and resolve to lay aside a small weekly or annual sum for the casualties and necessities of life.

A prolific cause of pecuniary embarrassment and domestic disagreement in many families is, the giving of frequent parties. They involve large expenses, both directly and incidentally. They excite discontent, pride, envy, and other evil passions. I do not say these consequences are the necessary fruits of social parties; I merely describe them as they exist in society generally.

A lady, for example, decides, in concert with her husband, to have a party. Who shall be invited is the first question. The husband objects to one, the wife to another. One family is omitted from prejudice, another from pride, a third because they did not invite them to their last social gathering. Thus, if the husband and wife make out the list without a positive disagreement, they bring a variety of improper emotions into action, and are made morally worse.

The next thing will be to prepare the house for the reception of the invited guests. In doing this, the lady is reminded of some defect in the style, or deficiency in the quantity of her furniture. She will then greet her husband, on his return from his place of business, with a request of this sort, "My dear, don't you think we need a sofa for our front parlour?"

"No, Ellen, I do not. Our parlour

looks very well now; and I cannot afford to purchase a sofa at present."

"But you know that the Ellingtons have a beautiful sofa in their parlour; and when they come to our house, our furniture will look mean in their eyes. A sofa would add very much to the appearance of the front parlour."

"It would look very well, Ellen; but we do not need it. We have a very good sofa in the back parlour; and, so long as we are satisfied, we must not care about the opinions of the Ellingtons or any one else."

"I do not care a great deal about the opinions of others, Henry; but I do like to appear as well as my neighbours: and I don't think I shall enjoy the party unless you get me a new sofa."

The dialogue proceeds, and the result is, that Ellen succeeds in overcoming the scruples of her husband. The front parlour is graced by the presence of a new and fashionable sofa.

But Ellen is not yet satisfied. Another of her friends, she recollects, had a beautiful set of girandoles on the mantel. They were greatly admired by the company present: for the first time she perceives that her own mantel looks very bare; she certainly *must* have the girandoles. As before, the reluctant husband consents, and the desired ornaments are brought home.

Thus prepared, the party is given. Ellen and her husband labour hard to entertain the company. Several hours are passed in the confusion of mixed conversation, in which the characters, dress, and circumstances of their acquaintances are pretty thoroughly discussed; but it would be difficult to find a single person who is in the least benefited. The evening has been passed in idle and frivolous conversation, altogether beneath the dignity of the Christian character, and the visitors have therefore suffered harm.

Ellen is much chagrined; for amidst the confusion of tongues, she thought she heard some one censure her for extravagance, and for *looking up in the world*, on account of the sofa and girandoles. Henry is in no better mood, for the expenses have much exceeded their estimate, and he is fearful of embarrassment in his business.

Such is the history of vast numbers of parties; and if the newly married intend to be economical, and to live a happy life, let them resolve not to fall into this habit. There is no religious profit to be derived from social parties; but, on the contrary, much evil to be suffered. Seek your pleasure at home. Depend on your own resources for enjoyment. Books, rational conversation, and the occasional presence of a *few* select friends, to pass an evening by your fireside, will furnish unfailing sources of innocent pleasure, without resorting to the fashionable, but evil custom of giving large parties. And as to the senseless charge of being unfashionable, you must treat it with profound and silent contempt.

A corresponding independence of action in regard to dress, servants, &c., must be maintained if you determine to prosper. Study to be happy within your own circle; make that a "dear domestic round," and the "enchanting circle," and it will be of small consequence to you who sneers without.

Among the quaint sayings of the immortal Franklin are these: "At a great pennyworth pause awhile;" and, "Many have been ruined by buying good pennyworths;" and again, "Buy what thou hast no need of, and ere long thou shalt sell thy necessaries." These proverbs are directed against a most ruinous practice among many housekeepers of *buying a thing because it is cheap.* There is ruin in this habit; for nothing is *cheap* that you do not really want. Avoid it, therefore, and adopt as a rule in your domestic economy, "We will never purchase what we do not really want."

If the young bride and bridegroom will

seriously study these practical hints, and resolutely reduce them to practice, they can hardly fail to prosper in the affairs of this life. Remember the saying of Franklin, the Solomon of his age, that, "They that will not be counselled cannot be helped;" and again, "If you will not hear reason, she will surely rap your knuckles."

CHAPTER VII.

On making Home Happy.

The first year of married life *usually* decides its character for weal or woe. During that time the parties either assimilate and accommodate their different characteristics to each other, or else they beget a progeny of animosities, prejudices, and differences, which embitter the rest of their lives. The newly married should, therefore, diligently cultivate the delicate plant of conjugal love, that it may grow into a thrifty tree, beneath whose pleasant shadow they may peacefully rest in after years; and with whose delicious fruit they may refresh their spirits in the great battle of life. Neglect or indifference *now* may shed a fatal influence on the future; for,

"Soon fades the rose; once past the fragrant hour,
 The loiterer finds a bramble for a flower."

I will suppose that you are now comfortably settled in your bridal home. Your house is suitably, perhaps elegantly furnished. Everything wears an aspect of beauty and neatness, and you both feel a high sense of satisfaction in being the possessors of such a home. This is well; it is cause for much gratitude to your heavenly Father; but remember what has been hinted before, *outward comforts alone will not make home happy.* There are many stately halls, many magnificent mansions, whose arches and walls echo to the sighs of their unhappy owners: many homes, abounding even with riches, where the wretched couple sleep in different apartments, and loathe the chain which binds them to dwell together beneath the same roof. And there is many a cottage, bare of elegance, scarcely comfortable, in which domestic bliss sits joyously enthroned. A home is made happy, therefore, by the *spirit* of those who compose it, and not by the amount of outward comforts it possesses.

I have somewhere read of a bridegroom who gloried in his eccentricities. He requested his bride to accompany him into the garden, a day or two after their wedding. He then threw a line over the roof of their cottage; giving his wife one end of the line, he retreated to the other side, and exclaimed, "Pull the line!"

She pulled it, at his request, as far as she could. He cried, "Pull it over!"

"I can't," she replied.

"But pull with all your might," shouted the whimsical young husband.

But vain were all the efforts of the bride to pull over the line, so long as her husband held on to the opposite end. But when he came round, and they both pulled at one end, it came over with great ease.

"There!" said he, as the line fell from the roof; "you see how hard and ineffectual was our labour when we pulled in opposition to each other; but how easy and pleasant it was when we pulled together.

It will be thus with us, my dear, through life. If we oppose each other, it will be hard work; if we act together, it will be pleasant to live. Let us always pull together."

This homely illustration contains the true philosophy of a happy home. Neither of you *alone* can make your new home completely happy. I am not a convert to the doctrine of an inscription said to have been engraved on an ancient wedding-ring. "One quiet, both happy," was the motto. Doubtless, the quietude and propriety of one will do much toward the creation of a blissful home; but sorrow will be there, unless both husband and wife contribute liberally to the object. To this end, the labour must be mutual. Both must persist in diffusing a sweet spirit through its atmosphere, and the work will be accomplished.

You must, above all other things, divest yourselves of SELFISHNESS, which is the sure extinguisher of love; since "confidence cannot dwell where SELFISHNESS is porter at the gate." It must be the labour of each to promote and to *prefer* the happiness of the other. "The marriage contract," says a great moral philosopher, (Wayland,) "binds each party, whenever individual gratification is concerned, to prefer the happiness of the other party to its own. If pleasure can be enjoyed by both, the happiness of both is increased by enjoying it in common. If it can be enjoyed but by one, each should prefer that it be enjoyed by the other. And if there be sorrow to be endured, or inconvenience to be suffered, each should desire, if possible, to bear the infliction for the sake of shielding the other from pain."

This is one of the grand secrets of domestic bliss. Nothing is more destructive to real affection than to be always receiving and never returning kindnesses, for, "such is the nature of the human affections, that we derive a higher and a purer pleasure from rendering happy those whom we love than from self-gratification. **Thus, a parent prefers self-denial, for the sake of a child, to self-indulgence.** The same principle is illustrated in every case of pure and **disinterested** benevolence. This is **the essential element** on which depends **the happiness of the married state.** To be in the highest degree happy, we must **each** prefer the happiness of another to our **own."** —*Wayland's Moral Science.*

But what shall one do if the other betrays a spirit of selfishness, and does not contribute to the bliss of home? In this case the injured party will require great patience and strong resolution to maintain a self-denying position—to do the duties of a true affection without the encouragements of a reciprocated love. But difficult as this task may be, it will be really easier in practice than to return neglect by reproof, or indifference by complaint. Patient perseverance in the duties of an unselfish affection, will have its effect on a selfish companion; perhaps it may *in the end* illustrate the motto of the old wedding-ring, "*One quiet, both happy.*"

Let me suppose a case, by way of illustrating the operation of selfishness in one of its forms.

CONRAD is a lawyer by profession, a resident in a populous city, and quite successful in his toilsome profession. He is married to a lady, who makes what the world calls a good wife; and several years have passed without any very serious difficulty between them. True, they could not claim the far-famed "flitch of bacon." Yet no fierce storms have disturbed the serenity of their matrimonial sky. Four healthy children stand like thrifty "olive plants" round their table, and they are happy, probably, beyond the ordinary lot of families.

With all this, however, the thistle mars the beauty of their family garden. Conrad's wife, MATILDA, with all her amiability, is strongly selfish. She cannot endure the privations of maternal life without frequent bursts of complaint; and there is nothing so annoying to her feelings as to have Conrad seek a recreation in which she cannot share. He has, of course, learned this long since, and has, in consequence, often denied himself those relaxations which were necessary to his health, rather than awaken the displeasure of Matilda.

But the toils of his profession are wearing away his energies. He feels the absolute necessity of repose, and determines to spend a week or two of the summer in visiting the Falls of Niagara. Going home one afternoon, after he has matured his plans, he addresses his wife something after the following manner:—

"Matilda, my health is failing under the continued toil of business. I must seek some relief, or I shall be sick."

"I think you *are* labouring too severely for your health. Why don't you rest a little, Conrad?"

"That is what I have been thinking

about; and I have concluded to spend a week or two in visiting Niagara."

"Well, I will go too. It will do us all good to get away from the city this hot weather."

"But, surely, you do not think of taking the children on so long a tour. Consider the fatigue they will occasion. If you will leave them at home, I will most gladly take you for the trip."

"No, indeed; I will not leave my children at home. I should not take any comfort. Something might happen to them during our absence, and that would make me feel very wretched."

"But, Matilda, your sister will take your place, and do all that you would for them. And, surely, if our health demands a brief departure from the cares of home, we may trust our little ones to the care of God."

"If the children cannot go, Conrad, I will not; and I am sure I do not wish to be left at home while *you* are seeking *your* pleasure abroad."

"That is an unkind remark, Matilda. I would gladly have your company if you would go under proper circumstances. If you will not, then certainly you ought to consent to my doing what may be necessary for my health."

"You can rest at home as well as at Niagara, if you choose; only you want to get away, and are willing to leave me, sick or well, to be confined like a prisoner to the house."

Matilda was, by this time, quite sour in her spirit. Conrad saw that if he took his intended journey, it would occasion bitterness between him and his wife. He therefore yielded to his Matilda, who, triumphing in her conquest, little thought that, though she had won him to her selfish wishes, she had lost what was worth more to her than a year's absence—HIS RESPECT.

The conduct of MADAME CATHARINE ADORNA, an Italian lady of distinguished piety, furnishes a beautiful illustration of the power of an unselfish affection to subdue a selfish nature. "She was united in marriage to a person of high rank, whose temper and habits were so entirely unsuited to her own as to render her situation exceedingly trying, and to deprive her of all happiness in that relation."*

Madame Adorna received this trial in a truly heroic spirit. She bore the outbreaks of her husband's temper with Christian submission; she devoted herself to the task of making his home attractive and delightful. And she had her reward: for "her husband's heart relented. He saw and felt the difference, the vast difference, between himself and a true Christian. God gave her the satisfaction, in answer to her fervent prayers, attended with appropriate personal efforts, to see her husband an humbled, penitent, and altered man. . . . . And he continued in these humble and happy dispositions till the period of his departure from the world, which took place soon after.'

* Life of Madame Catharine Adorna, by Professor Upham.

It is indispensable to a blissful home that the husband provide for the supply of his family with a liberality proportioned to his means, and to a judicious economy. He that provideth not for his own household, according to an inspired judge, *is worse than an infidel*. A mean, niggardly husband is sure to win the scorn of his wife, unless she is a very superior, pious woman. The mutual confidence in financial matters I have already counselled, will go far to prevent this frequent evil. Yet, even with explanations, and good understanding of circumstances, it often happens that a stingy husband gives great uneasiness to his wife. I have known some such to allow a weekly sum for the expenses of the table, and then constantly fret and complain because the style of living was simple, and in keeping with the allowance. Such conduct is contemptible, and cannot fail to destroy domestic peace.

But how shall I designate those indolent men who neglect to make suitable provision for their families, and thus compel their high-spirited and energetic wives to labour like slaves in order to maintain a respectable appearance. There is a meanness in such conduct that is beneath contempt; and the man who is guilty of it deserves to be banished from civilized society.

I have several such husbands in my recollections of past life. I will outline the features of one of them, on the same principle that led our ancestors to leave the malefactor dangling in his chains on the highway. They hoped thereby to make crime a terror to the living.

Young ALEXANDER was a mechanic, of respectable parentage, and fair talents. His habits were free from all vices but that of indolence. He was late at his shop in the morning; ever complaining of being weary, and, like Goldsmith's "Prince Bonbennin," was always ready to be amused with trifles. Notwithstanding all this, Alexander won the affections of the amiable MARIA, and married her. True, many, who knew Alexander best, trembled for the happiness of Maria; but, as his character stood fair, and his friends were highly respected, they said nothing.

For the first year or two the young couple did very well. Their expenses were small, for Maria had a plentiful wardrobe of her own, and Alexander's relatives gave them an occasional present. But at length his parents died. Two children increased the cost of living very materially; and it became obvious that Alexander's resources, without some increase of effort, were insufficient to support his family. Then came embarrassments and trials. They could not pay their rent; Maria needed a dress to appear in abroad, and could not obtain it. Alexander himself was growing shabby in his appearance. Everything bore the marks of decaying circumstances.

Here, then, was a summons to act with the energy of a man. Alexander, by being prompt in the morning, and by working every day with ordinary diligence, could easily place himself above embarrassment. Maria gently pleaded with him, but in vain. He would still persist in sleeping away his morning hours: a slight indisposition made him drop his tools, and lounge away the day in an adjoining store. A political meeting, a parade of soldiers or firemen, always witnessed him among the spectators; and not unfrequently he spent a day with hook and line, on an adjacent pond.

His affairs, of course, grew worse and worse. His wife saw the impending ruin; and, failing to bestir the energies of the indolent Alexander, she set out to do, by her own skill and industry, what he ought to have done. Being well skilled in the use of the needle, she took in sewing, and, with the patient toil for which woman is distinguished, laboured by day, and far into every night, for her support. She soon succeeded in paying their debts, in clothing herself and children, and in contributing to the current expenses of the family. Since then, by the continuance of her labours, they have enjoyed the comforts of life; but Maria is toiling at the expense of life. She grows old rapidly. Her hair is turning prematurely gray. She looks oppressed, care-worn, sad; though she never complains. Her unmanly husband is the witness of this decay; but remains the same indolent, easy, and, may I not truly say, *unfaithful* husband. When Maria dies, he will be guilty of her blood; since his neglect to provide for her wants will unquestionably shorten her life.

I cannot help despising the meanness of Alexander. The reader cannot. He is despicable beyond the power of words to describe. Then, young husband, be fixed never to resemble Alexander; but, to the best of your ability, provide liberally for her whom you have taken to your bosom, and for the children God may be pleased to give you.

Let me also guard you against an evil spirit, that as surely destroys the peace of married life as the moth does a woollen garment; I mean the disposition to fret at, and to find fault with each other.

Some husbands, after being vexed and tried in their business, go home with a sour temper, and breathe out their anger in surly complaints. The dinner is poor, or not cooked to their tastes; or it cost too much. Something is wrong, because they are determined to have it so: and thus the atmosphere of home is dreary and wretched. The wife is disheartened, and her soul is sad.

In other families, the offender is the wife. The moment her husband enters the room his ears are annoyed by a volley of complaints. The foibles of the domestic, the faults of the children, the toil of housekeeping, the little daily mishaps of life, together with a thousand and one imaginary trials, are all rained down upon his hapless head, stinging him like a shower of needles, irritating his temper, and gradually, but surely, creating a disgust of home, and an alienation of heart from his wife. A woman may imagine that she is justified in the indulgence of such a temper; she may hope for exact compliance from her husband. But such imaginations are idle, such hopes folly. It would be as reasonable to place a perishing infant beneath the pelting winter storm for resuscitation. No! The only effect of fretting and scolding in a wife is to render herself disgusting to her husband, and to blight the delicate flower of conjugal affection.

DANTE has given his scolding wife, GEMMA, an unenviable immortality in his "Inferno." It is generally admitted that he alludes to her in the following lines, which he puts into the mouth of a lost soul:—

"—— Me, my wife,
Of savage temper, more than aught beside,
Hath to this evil brought."

This is a terrible stroke on the temper of Gemma; yet not too severe: for, alas! many men have been brought to ruin in two worlds by the bitterness of fault-finding, scolding, fretful wives.

ROUSSEAU has elegantly said:—"The empire of woman is an empire of softness, of address, of complacency. Her commands are caresses, her menaces are tears;" and a living writer (Rev. Dr. Barnes) says,—A sweet temper, daily maintained, is more precious than great exploits; it is like the budding spring which flows gently; it is like the little rivulet gliding through the meadow, and running along day and night before the farm-house, which is far more useful than the foaming cataract. One Niagara is sufficient for the world, while it needs tens of thousands of rivulets to water its farms and gardens, and to flow on continually and everywhere. An inspired writer, with still greater beauty, has also said of a truly virtuous and dutiful wife, that "She openeth her mouth with wisdom, and in her tongue is the law of kindness;" while of the scolding wife he has written, "The contentions of a wife are a continual dropping;" upon which the learned Bishop Patrick has this comment:—She "drives a man to undo his family himself, when he is no more able to live at home with her, than to dwell in a rotten and ruinous house, through the roof of which the rain drops perpetually."

Resolve, then, young wife, to endure any amount of suffering, of toil, and even of injury, rather than to become a fretful, ill-tempered woman. Be sweet-tempered. Do not listen to those unthinking women who tell you you will be trampled upon unless you assert your rights, and speak for yourself. You cannot gain true ascendency over a man by ill temper, but by gentleness you may. Men find so little sincere friendship abroad, so little true sympathy in the selfish world, that they gladly yield themselves to the influence of a gentle spirit at home. Mrs. Hemans has beautifully written the sentiment of many a weary-hearted husband in the following spirited lines:—

> "Thou hast a charmed cup, O fame!
>   A draught that mantles high;
> And seems to lift this earthly frame
>   Above mortality.
> Away! to me—a woman—bring
> Sweet water from affection's spring.
>
> "Thou hast a voice whose thrilling tone
>   Can bid each life-pulse beat,
> As when a trumpet's note hath blown,
>   Calling the brave to meet:
> But mine, let mine—a woman's breast,
> By words of home-born love be bless'd."

Seek, then, young bride, to secure the calm bliss, which, like some sweet aromatic plant, now diffuses its sweet odours through the chambers of your home, by gentleness of spirit. She is the truly happy wife,—

> "She that makes the humblest hearth
> Lovely but to one on earth."

Nor is the young husband to neglect the same spirit. It must be his ambition so to live, if it be possible, with the chosen of his affection, that, if called to close her eyes in death, her dying lips may adopt the address of the expiring Vaudois wife to her husband:—

> "I bless thee for kind looks and words
>   Shower'd on my path like dew ;
> For all the love in those deep eyes,
>   A gladness ever new ;
> For the *voice which ne'er to mine replied*
>   But in kindly tones of cheer ;
> For every spring of happiness
>   My soul hath tasted here."—Mrs. Hemans

CHAPTER VIII.

On Conformity to Circumstances.

I ONCE called on a lady, whom I found in tolerable health, and in very comfortable pecuniary circumstances. But a cloud was on her brow, and a burden on her heart. She complained of depression of spirits; of loss of spiritual comfort, of great discouragement.

I dislike all approaches to impertinent meddling with the grief of others, even in a pastor. But here was a case in which counsel would avail nothing without some knowledge of the cause of her sadness. I therefore told her to adopt the question of David, and inquire, "*Why* art thou cast down, O my soul? *Why* art thou disquieted within me?" Upon this she readily divulged the secret of her sorrow, by remarking, "I am home-sick. I do not like living in this town. I shall never be happy until I get back to ——."

"But you have your husband and children here with you; and does not their presence make *this* your home?" I replied.

"Yes," said she, "they are here, and my husband is doing well in his business; but I shall never be contented until we move back to ——."

"But you surely would not have your husband abandon a profitable business, and go back to a place where he was not so fortunate, merely to gratify your feeling of home-sickness?" I replied.

"I know it is hard to ask him to do it; but stay here I cannot, and be happy," was her reply, accompanied with signs of deep feeling.

I said what occurred to me as the most suitable advice, and, after commending her to God in prayer, left her with a sincere pity for her exceeding weakness and childishness of mind. It was not a great while before she succeeded in inducing her husband to break up his business, and to leave the town.

This was certainly very reprehensible conduct on the part of a wife. It displayed a weakness of intellect unworthy of a woman; a want of self-control unworthy of a Christian; and a want of submission unworthy of an affectionate wife. How must her perpetual entreaties to her husband to remove, have chafed and grieved his spirit! How he must have despised that wife in his heart for her weakness and want of love to him! How severe the toil, and oppressive the care, to which he was subjected through her whim! If he subsequently proved unsuccessful, and want invaded their home, how painful the reflections of that wife! Viewed on every side, her discontent has no excuse; it was her *duty* as a wife to cheerfully submit to the necessities of her husband's business. In her marriage covenant, she had vowed to give herself to him; to exchange her early home for his, and to identify herself with all his interests. Instead of being thus faithful, she deliberately sacrificed *his* interests to *her* feelings.

In beautiful contrast with this unwomanly conduct, I present the example of the devoted and amiable Mrs. HANNAH M. PICKARD.* She had married a gentleman whose sphere of professional labour lay in New-Brunswick, far away from her native and beloved Boston. After a brief residence in her new home, she was spending a few weeks in the vicinity of her natal city with her relatives. It was quite natural for a lady of her intense and delicate affections to desire, under such circumstances, to live near her native home. She had such a wish, but, with the true heroism of woman, she suppressed it for her husband's sake. The following extract from one of her letters to Mr. Pickard, exhibits the feelings of a truly devoted and Christian wife. She is speaking of Chelsea, where she was then visiting:—

"The Methodist society here," she writes,

* See her Memoir, by Rev. E. Otheman

"is at present, as it has been the greater part of the winter, favoured with an encouraging spirit of revival. They have a very neat new chapel, to which, by the way, there are many thoughts among a *circle* of the members of inviting *you*. I find they are half ready, in New-England, to *claim* you on more than one account. They seem to calculate upon your coming among them, I find, though not from any encouragement or word received from me. Whatever may be my private feelings, my lips, I am purposed, shall not transgress in this matter. Far be it from me. *I would not, if I could, withdraw one glance of yours from the strait and narrow way of duty.*"

It is easy to see the superiority of such a wife over the one in my previous etching; and how much more happy she would make her admiring husband. She would also increase his *respect* for her character, which, by the way, is a very important object for a wife who would be happy, since love cannot outlive the loss of esteem.

While some ladies are uneasy because they cannot live *where* they desire, others are discontented with the condition or profession of their husbands. They are *too poor* to live in a style suited to their tastes, or their professions have some circumstances connected with them not agreeable to their feelings. Hence, they set themselves in opposition to their husbands' pursuits, and determine to be unhappy until they abandon them. No peace or rest is permitted to the doomed man whose capricious partner thus determines to hunt him from his profession. Complainings, fretfulness, censures, tears, become the incessant annoyances of his home, until his tried soul grows weary of life; his evenings are spent in company, and, if strong religious or moral principles do not bind him to the proprieties of life, he falls into vices, and thus brings swift ruin upon himself and family.

It is more than probable that a minister's bride may see these pages. To her these hints on being content with the profession of her husband are all-important, both on account of the varied and perplexing trials of the life she has chosen, and because of the high and awful responsibilities connected with the work to which her companion is called.

JOHN WESLEY had the misfortune to marry a lady who did not and would not sympathize with him in the great duties of his profession. His almost continual absence from home, his correspondence with pious females, his preference of duty to ease, to self-indulgence, and even to her wishes, excited her jealousy, her anger, and even her persecuting spirit. The burden of soul her unwomanly conduct imposed on that laborious man of God, had no witness who could comprehend its magnitude but Jehovah. It was such that, as is well known, he ceased to live with her. Instead of being a help meet for him in the battle of life, she was an insupportable trial, and, but for the unsurpassed energy of his noble soul, would have been a sad hindrance to his gigantic labours.

In delightful contrast let me present the minister's bride with a view of the lovely CATHARINE VON BORA, the affectionate wife of MARTIN LUTHER. Educated in a nunnery, she had but little opportunity to prepare herself for the duties of domestic life. Unused to the strifes and storms of public life, which broke so fiercely over the reformer's head, it would not have been surprising if she had sunk in terror beneath their fury. But Catharine was the possessor of the highest and noblest qualities of her sex; and, like a true wife, she devoted herself to the happiness of her chosen lord. She gave a realization to the poet's doctrine, "*to bless is to be blest;*" for in contributing to the happiness of her great husband, she found this grand secret of domestic bliss, and awakened an overflowing spring of joy in her own bosom. Luther loved her with the ardent affection of his noble nature. "I love my Catharine," he said; "I love her more than myself: for I would sooner die than see any harm happen to her or to her children."

Which is the pleasing portrait? Does the young bride admire the jealous, selfish wife of Wesley, placing herself, with her whims and fancies, in the path of his usefulness, like a sharp thorn, until she compelled that patient man to forsake her? Or does she prefer the more amiable Catharine, entering into the great plans of her noble husband; soothing his chafed spirit by her gentleness; cheering his desponding heart with her eloquent applications of holy writ; and finding her own enjoyment in his happiness? I know she condemns the former; she admires the latter. She will, therefore, form her own character after the model of Catharine, and studiously, resolutely, conform herself to the requirements of her husband's profession.

The only way for the young wife to do this effectually is, to enter into the spirit of her husband's vocation. The bride of a merchant or mechanic will find this a necessary part of her duty; but nothing can atone for its absence in the wife of a minister of Christ.

She must learn to appreciate the obligations that bind her husband to his work. Preaching Christ is not so much his profession as his vocation. He has not entered upon it as men select one mode of support in preference to another. He has been called to it by the Holy Ghost; and if so called, he cannot abandon it without bringing down the "woe unto me if I preach not the Gospel" upon his devoted head. The interests involved in his work are momentous beyond conception. Immortal destinies are linked to his labours. Human salvation depends on his fidelity, for if God has called him into the pulpit, it is because his eye discerns an instrumental adaptation in him, to some part of the great work of human redemption. It is not saying too much to affirm, that on his continuance in the work of the ministry hangs the eternal fate of some of the creatures of God.

The minister's bride must study to feel the grandeur of her husband's mission. She must view it in its relation to the sublime plan of redemption. She must gaze on the majestic results growing out of his labours. She must view, by the eye of faith, the endless gratitude of the souls who will become the seals of her husband's ministry, and, above all, she must tremble before the idea of *dragging her husband out of the pulpit into hell!* Let her never forget that no man's salvation is in greater peril than that of the minister, who, through the lust of money, the love of indolence, or the persuasions of a wife, leaves his appropriate sphere, and buries himself in the obscurity of private life. Alas! how many of those ministers who have quitted their vocation have fallen victims to worldliness and sin!

With such ideas as these working in her heart, the minister's wife will never tease her husband to locate. She will not fill his ears, and grieve his heart, by peevish complaints about the hardships of her lot. No: but with heroic courage she will endure her trials for the sake of Christ, knowing that her inheritance in glory will be enlarged by her participation in the difficulties of her husband's calling. The physical ills entailed by the migratory life of the itinerant; the mental torture caused by the frequent sundering of friendly ties; the unceasing care for the Church of Christ which burdens her, through sympathy with her husband; the unkind and uncharitable conduct of lukewarm professors, will all be cheerfully accepted from Christ as a portion of that cup which *He* deems proper to apply to her lips. She will drink it in *hope;* she will endure all, like her great Exemplar, who "*for the joy that was set before him*, endured the cross, despising the shame, and is set down at the right hand of the throne of God."

This is motive enough, for there is joy

set before the faithful wife who is a help *meet* for a minister of Jesus Christ. She may, and doubtless will, have cause to weep and suffer; but her tears are neither lost nor forgotten. A drop of water, falling into the shell of an obscure fish, becomes in due time a pearl of beauty on the brow of royalty; so shall her tears, dropping from eyes of sadness, and flowing from an agonized heart, be carefully gathered up, and in the happy future be brought forth, changed to pearls of unfading whiteness, and wrought into that "crown of life" which Christ will give her in THAT DAY. Of all the disciples of Christ, the minister's wife should be the first to repose on the delightful assurance, that "these light afflictions, which are but for a moment, shall work out for us *a far more exceeding* and eternal weight of glory."

May I not hope that the dear lady whose eye now reads this page, and who is the bride of a "preacher of righteousness," will record a covenant with Christ to be all to her husband in his profession that Christ can desire! Resolve to catch the inspiration of his mission by study and prayer; to heroically endure your peculiar trials for Jesus' sake: to sympathize with your husband in every part of his labours,—in his studies, his pastoral duties, his public efforts. Resolve to stimulate his zeal, to remind him of the principles and aims of his vocation; and, in a word, to be as the guardian angel of his spirit. Resolve neither to do nor to be aught that will detract from his influence. Do these things, young bride, and though by your *direct* effort a soul may never bless you as its converter, yet thousands shall call you blessed for the influence of your spirit on your husband's success. Verily, you shall have your reward. Your husband will esteem you; the Church will embalm you in its memories, and God will honour you.

Let me, before leaving this point, refer you to that touching exhibition of conjugal esteem made at Bath a few years since.

It was the jubilee of the ordination of the venerable and eloquent William Jay. For fifty years he had ministered to that admiring flock, and, as a tribute of love, the ladies of his church presented him with a purse containing over three thousand dollars. His wife was present in that vast assemblage. He took the purse, and, presenting it to her, said,—

"I take this purse, and present it to you, madam,—to you, madam, who have always kept my purse; and therefore it has been so well kept. Consider it entirely sacred,—for your use, your service, your benefit. I feel this to be unexpected by you, but it is perfectly deserved."

Then addressing the audience, he added: "I am sure there is not one here but would acquiesce in this if he knew the value of this female as a wife for more than fifty years. I must mention the obligation the public are under to her, if I have been enabled to serve my generation: how much my Church and congregation owe to her watchings over their pastor's health, whom she has cheered under all his trials, and reminded of his duties, while she animated him in their performance: how often she has wiped the evening dews from his forehead, and freed him from interruptions and embarrassments, that he might be free for his work! She, too, is the mother of another mother in America, who has reared thirteen children, all of whom are walking with her in the way everlasting."

How must the bosom of that noble wife have heaved with almost unearthly joy as this deserved eulogy dropped from her husband's lips! O, the bliss of a life was compressed into that moment! And such a bliss may be yours, young bride. Not perhaps under like circumstances, but before that august assembly where you and your husband shall receive your final reward. Then your husband, viewing his crown, radiant with stars, shall gaze upon its brightness, and think, perchance, how much, under Christ, it owes its adornments to you. And you, I repeat, "shall not lose your reward."

But if you pursue an opposite course; if you vex your husband's soul by discontent; if you add to his burdens, instead of making them lighter; if you unfit him for his work by the peevishness of your temper,—you cripple his energies, discourage his heart, and succeed in teasing him into a location; you shall also have your reward. You shall see God *set his face against you and him:* domestic bitterness will poison your enjoyments; misfortunes will haunt your steps; God will curse you in soul and in body, and in all probability both you and he will fail of heaven. O then, beware, young bride, how you treat your husband's high vocation. It is from God; and it is a very solemn thing to trifle with the callings of the Almighty.

Let not the husband imagine, because I have written thus to the young wife, that he has nothing to do in assisting her to conform to the circumstances of his condition or profession. It is not sufficient for you to provide her with the best home which your means permit. That she had before; and you would do as much as this for your housekeeper; and it is *rarely* that domestic unhappiness grows solely out of external circumstances. I agree with COLERIDGE, who says: "Show me one couple unhappy merely on account of their limited circumstances, and I will show you ten who are wretched from other causes." Doubtless many a wife owes the growth of her discontent to the absence of appropriate sympathy with the trials of her new situation on the part of her husband.

"Sympathy," says MOUNTFORD, in his "Marriage Sermon," "is an essential of the human heart. There is many a soul of noble capacities lying in sluggish darkness for want of some word out of itself, some human tone, some little encouragement, and that, perhaps, so slight, that even a child might utter it. Others there are, who are awake to righteousness, to all the lofty attainments that are possible therein on this earth, who revolve in their minds many plans of good, and who yet make no progress, for want of a quickening impulse external from themselves. . . . This want of sympathy, this dependence on external help, is God's appointment; it is our nature; it is incidental to us social creatures; it is an ordained occasion for the infusion of faith and energy into the soul, and which, at the same time, carry along with them an increase of love, a contributary effect of the conversational channel through which they flow."

The husband must remember this doctrine, and prevent his wife's fall into discontent and peevishness, by manifested sympathy with the first difficulties of her new situation. Is she perplexed with her domestic cares? Is she lonesome during the long hours of his necessary absence from home? Does her health give way under the peculiar conditions of her state? Are her indulgences fewer, and is her home less elegant, than in the days of her happy and thoughtless girlhood? Let the husband feel for her, and kindly express those feelings; let him whisper words of encouragement in her ears; let him show her that her efforts to adapt herself to his circumstances are appreciated, and he will probably awaken that ardent devotedness to his happiness which has so often characterized her sex.

Remember, young husband, that "the soul of woman lives in love."

> "And shouldst thou, wondering, mark a tear
>   Unconscious from her eyelids break,
> Be pitiful, and soothe the fear
>   That strong man's heart may ne'er partake."

Should you even fail of success, owing to the unfortunate absence of truly noble qualities in her character, you will at least feel the high satisfaction of knowing that, in your misfortune, you are blameless. But fail wholly, you cannot. Sympathy will make some impression even on the most selfish natures; and you may develop the highest qualities of woman in your bride, and realize in your marriage history the ideal of the poet, painted in these beautiful lines of BRAINARD:—

> "I saw two clouds at morning
>   Tinged with the rising sun;
> And in the dawn they floated on,
>   And mingled into one;
> I thought that morning cloud was blest,
> It moved so sweetly to the west.
>
> "I saw two summer currents
>   Flow smoothly to their meeting,
> And join their course, with silent force,
>   In peace each other greeting;
> Calm was their course, through banks of green,
> While dimpling eddies play'd between.
>
> "Such be your gentle motion,
>   Till life's last pulse shall beat;
> Like summer's beam and summer's stream,
>   Float on, in joy, to meet
> A calmer sea, where storms shall cease,—
> A purer sky, where all is peace."

CHAPTER IX.
Of Domestic Servants.

SERVANTS have often been called "*great plagues:*" a saying which most housekeepers will readily endorse. There are few families that hire "help" but find it a source of much vexation and trial. It was so in the days of Abraham and Lot, whose hired men quarrelled; it is so now, and will continue to be so while man remains in his fallen state. The reason, I apprehend, is **this**: the relation of master and servant is an effect of sin—a portion of the curse which blights our joys, and converts this world into a vale of tears. For it was *sin* that caused the debility, idleness, or luxury on the one side, and the dependence and poverty on the other, which make the relations of master and servant necessary to the existence of social life. It must, therefore, be endured as a "necessary evil."

I would advise the newly married to do

without help *if possible*. If a simple style of living, systematic arrangements, and a little occasional aid, will enable the young wife to dispense with a "hired girl," let her be dispensed with by all means. A servant brings greatly increased expenses, a new moral element, new cares and new responsibilities into a family. If happiness, if genuine domestic enjoyment, is the object of the newly married, they will certainly avoid hiring help, except in the extremity of necessity.

The *expense* of a servant is a question worthy of some consideration from the newly married. It is not the item of *wages* merely, though that is considerable, but the cost of board, of waste, and frequently of the dishonesty of the help, that makes the question of expense a serious one. Says a writer on this subject:—

"Besides the wages, board, and lodging of a female servant, there must be a fire exclusively for her, or else she must sit with the family, and hear every word that passes between them, or between them and their friends. Besides the blaze of coals, there is another sort of flame she will inevitably covet. In plain language, you have a *man* to keep, a part at least of every week: and the leg of lamb which might have lasted you and your wife three days, will by this gentleman's sighs be borne away in one. Shut the door against this intruder, and she will go out herself; nor will she always go empty handed."

The same writer speaks of having seen large quantities of food, fuel, &c., given away by servants early in the morning to their various friends. And what housekeeper of many years' experience has not been conscious of suffering by similar peculations!

Frequently a hired girl brings an unhappy moral element into the family. What misery is often caused by the fierce temper of a servant! The very presence of such a person infects the moral atmosphere. The outbreaks of her temper irritate and annoy the wife; she, in her turn, soured by the contagion, complains bitterly of "Betty" or "Molly" to her husband. He feels vexed and tried at meeting complaints and ill-temper where he was wont to meet smiles, and conceives a degree of dislike for his home,—a diminution of regard for his wife. Time increases the evil, until domestic dissensions crown the formidable column of vexations, rising from the pedestal of an ill-tempered servant.

The influence of a wicked domestic is still more potent in that family which has children among its members. The fact is unquestionable, that a servant's influence has ruined many a child. Ghost stories, licentious anecdotes, and even unchaste habits, have been taught by such domestics to the unwary children, until they have fallen victims to superstitious fears or destructive vices.

How necessary it is, therefore, for the young husband and wife to begin their married life without "hired help," if practicable. It is a question in which their happiness is involved: they must treat it as one of the serious things of life.

There are many families, I doubt not, who keep "help," and endure all its vexations, not from the inability of the wife to do without it, but from an idea that it is more respectable to keep a servant than to do without one. To such allow me to say, first, The idea is a false one. You are not respected one atom the more for keeping a servant by any *whose respect is worth having;* secondly, If any young couple are disposed to prefer an imaginary respectability to happiness, they deserve to be miserable.

But it is highly probable this work will fall into the hands of many brides, whose delicate health or previous education makes the assistance of servants imperiously necessary. To such I will offer a word or two of counsel.

Pious servants, young women truly devoted to God, are to be preferred to all others. I know such servants are rarely to be obtained. Still there are such in the community. They are domestic jewels; and, when found, ought to be treated according to their worth.

In the present state of society, however, most families are compelled to take Irish Catholics into their service, and it becomes a serious question how they are to be treated.

I have heard some persons say they would not keep a girl in their house who would not attend family prayer. Their argument is, that a master has a right to compel all under his roof to submit to his authority.

This is true on all questions which do not involve matters of conscience. Every head of a family is bound to require a good moral deportment from all his dependents, and to exert his strongest influence to win them to religion. He ought, also, to insist on the attendance of his servants at some place of religious worship on the Sabbath; and if they are Protestants, to require their presence at the domestic altar on pain of dismissal from his employment. Such servants *cannot* have conscientious scruples to plead, and must possess elements of character too dangerous to be retained in a Christian family, if unwilling to join in family worship.

But the Catholic servant is in a different relation. She, poor victim of error, is taught by her priest, who stands, *to her mind*, in the place of God, to regard her master's religion with horror. She believes it would be sin to join therein. So far as she is concerned, if left to herself, she would have no such objection; but her tyrannical priest, usurping authority over her conscience, forbids her to do so. Now, what is to be done? Shall the Christian require her to violate her sense of duty? Or shall he submit to the unpleasant necessity, and permit her to absent herself at the hour of worship?

"Thus to permit your servant's absence, is to submit to *priestly dictation* as to the government of your family," said a zealous agent of the Protestant Society to me one day. To a certain extent this is true, though it is rather the scruples of the servant than the dictation of the priest to which we submit. Yet what is to be done? Insist on her presence, and, if places are abundant, she will leave your employment, and you must then hire another of the same class, who will follow her example, and thus your family is endlessly perplexed: if places are not to be had readily, your girl may possibly comply, but with such a sense of your tyranny, for so she will consider it, as will entirely neutralize your object in requiring her presence.

The result of my experience on the subject of Catholic help is, that it is not best to *insist* on their being present at your family worship. Let them be kindly invited to do so: if they comply, well; if not, we must submit to it until some pious Protestant girl can be obtained in her place. As to how the heads of a family can best perform their religious duty to such help, I can hardly advise, except to say, that we should so deport ourselves in their presence as to compel the conviction that Protestantism is better than Catholicism; we should, if they can read, place the Holy Scriptures in their hands, and such other books as may be suited to instruct them; we may also, with suitable wisdom, endeavour to instruct them by conversation; though, such is their prejudice against us heretics, it is rarely we can affect them thus. Every Christian pair must do *what they can* to bring these poor deluded servants, who swarm our cities and towns, to the knowledge of Jesus Christ.

Hired help should always be treated kindly, and even respectfully. The mistress, while she preserves her own dignity, should endeavour to treat her girl so that she may not *feel* her servitude. To do this does not require excessive familiarity, but only a kind spirit expressed in respectful language. Even a *rebuke* for an obvious fault is more weighty when uttered with kindness and without temper, than when it is administered in the shape of what is misnamed a "*good scolding.*" It is not necessary to take a hired girl so closely into the bosom of a family as to give her a seat at your own table or your own fireside. This may be done where there exists a suitability of manners and characters. There are some pious and intelligent hired girls whom I would gladly treat in this way; but there are others, and they form the vast majority, whose constant presence would be a barrier to all profitable social intercourse. It should never be forgotten that in employing a *servant*, we are not hiring a *companion;* if, however, that servant should be found to combine the qualifications for both of these relations, her being a servant cannot justify the employer in refusing to treat her according to her worth; for, although no leveller, yet I can heartily join in the following stanza of the Scottish poet, (Burns:)—

"Then let us pray, that come it may,
  As come it will for a' that,
That sense and worth o'er all the earth
  May bear the gree, and a' that."

To have the wheels of domestic life run smoothly, the wife must establish a system to which everything must bend, and into which she must infuse activity and vigour of movement. There must be an established hour for each meal, a distinct routine for the various duties of the household; a proper distribution of the several parts of household labour, so that the work and order of each day shall be apparent beforehand. Above all, it is indispensable for the young housewife to superintend her own kitchen. She *must* give direction and energy to her help. She must rise superior to that most silly of all silly notions, that it is degrading in a wife to labour in her own household. This most stupid of ideas she must trample under her feet, and glory in resembling that beautiful portrait of a perfect wife drawn so graphically by the glowing pencil of King Solomon, in Prov. xxxi, 10–27.

The following *fact*, which is taken from a recent British publication, conveys its own moral on several points not elsewhere touched in this work, but which, in this polluted world, are important to be guarded against by all who would be happy.

Mr. A—— married Miss B——. They were about the same age, and apparently matched as well as paired. He had his infirmities: a weakly constitution, caused by early sickness, and a very common mental infirmity—vanity. She was kind, benevolent, social in her disposition, and was devotedly attached to him. So well suited were they to each other, that twenty years of their wedded life passed away in uninterrupted peace.

At first, their circumstances were moderate. Having no children, and her mother being a resident in her family, Mrs. A—— did without a servant. But after twenty years their fortunes were so much improved that a larger domestic establishment appeared necessary to their station in life. And this gave rise to the further necessity of having a servant to meet the additional labour.

This circumstance, strange as it may seem, grew into a domestic viper, whose deadly bite poisoned the remainder of their lives.

A quiet girl, ignorant, but strong and healthy, was obtained from the country. She was very poor also. Her clothes were unfit for her appearance as a servant. Mrs. A—— was a generous woman, and, in the goodness of her heart, she undertook to clothe the girl. And here she unwittingly did her unsophisticated servant a great injury. Not, to be sure, in clothing her; but in doing so improperly. She gave her clothes superior to her circumstances,— finery such as the poor child had never touched before. As a natural consequence, she was greatly lifted up by her altered appearance; she did not know herself:

the seeds of vanity were planted in her heart, and in due time they yielded their harvest of crime and sorrow.

Perhaps this fault of Mrs. A—— might not have so seriously affected her own happiness, had she not been the prey of another. She was extremely fond of social intercourse, and, in consequence, was frequently, very frequently, absent from her own house and table. Her husband, being partially an invalid, did not choose to accompany her; and, being remarkably good-natured, did not complain. But, as a result, he was necessarily much waited on by the country girl, now grown into a smart, handsome young woman. She was very attentive to his wishes; and he favoured her with kind words in return. The girl felt flattered; he increased his attentions, until, after Mrs. A.'s return from a trip to Bologne with her brother, which had kept her from home a month, she made discoveries that led to a separation from her husband which lasted ten years, when death put an end to the guilty career of Mr. A. and his paramour.

"This simple narrative," says its writer, "which is quite true, has many a parallel in every-day life. Evil may spring from the best intentions, when not guided by sound judgment and experience. Happy are they who can learn from the experience of others."

CONCLUDING NOTE.

And now, young and happy pair, having given you such hints and counsels as I thought expedient and necessary to your happiness, I wish you adieu! May the peace of Christ rest on your spirits! May Providence guide you safely through the mysteries of life! May Eternal Love elevate you to the endless joys of that marriage supper which will celebrate the final union of Christ with his Church! Amen and Amen!

THE END.

www.ingramcontent.com/pod-product-compliance
Lightning Source LLC
Chambersburg PA
CBHW020617300426
44113CB00007B/674